English Practice Year 5

Question Book

Giles Clare

Name _____

Schofield & Sims

Introduction

The **Schofield & Sims English Practice Year 5 Question Book** uses step-by-step practice to develop children's understanding of key English concepts. It covers every Year 5 objective in the 2014 National Curriculum programme of study.

The structure

This book is split into units, which are based on the key areas of the English curriculum for Year 5. These are:

- Grammar
- Punctuation
- Spelling
- Vocabulary
- Reading comprehension.

Each double-page spread follows a consistent 'Practise', 'Extend' and 'Apply' sequence designed to deepen and reinforce learning. Each objective also includes a 'Remember' box that reminds children of the key information needed to help answer the questions.

There are three reading comprehension units in this book. Each reading comprehension unit is linked by an overarching theme and includes a fiction, non-fiction and poetry text. Each text is accompanied by a set of comprehension questions, which practise reading skills such as inference, retrieval, summarising, prediction and analysis of word choice.

Additionally, a 'Writing skills' section allows children to apply the skills they have developed throughout the book in an extended writing task. The writing task is inspired by the themes covered in the reading comprehension texts and gives opportunities for children to showcase their creative writing.

At the back of the book, there is a 'Final practice' section. Here, mixed questions are used to check children's understanding of the knowledge and skills acquired throughout the book and identify any areas that need to be revisited.

A mastery approach

The **Primary Practice English** series follows a knowledge-based mastery approach. The books have a focus on learning with purpose to improve children's ability across all areas of English and to link learning in grammar, punctuation, spelling, vocabulary, reading and writing. There is frequent, varied practice and application of concepts to improve children's confidence when using their skills. A strong emphasis is given to vocabulary enrichment, reading for pleasure and reading stamina.

Assessment and checking progress

A 'Final practice' section is provided at the end of this book to check progress against the Year 5 English objectives. Children are given a target time of 45 minutes to complete this section, which is marked out of 30. Once complete, it enables them to assess their new knowledge and skills independently and to see the areas where they might need more practice.

Online answers

Answers for every question in this book are available to download from the **Schofield & Sims** website. The answers are accompanied by detailed explanations where helpful. There is also a progress chart, allowing children to track their learning as they complete each set of questions, and an editable certificate.

Contents

Unit 1: Grammar ... 4
Subjects, verbs and objects ... 4
Relative clauses ... 6
Modal verbs ... 8
Adverbials ... 10
Cohesion in writing ... 12
The perfect forms ... 14
Using tenses consistently ... 16
Adverbs of possibility ... 18
Expanded noun phrases ... 20

Unit 2: Punctuation ... 22
Parentheses ... 22
Commas for clarity ... 24

Unit 3: Spelling ... 26
Silent and unstressed letters ... 26
Homophones and near homophones ... 28
Base words ... 30
Tricky spellings ... 32
Prefixes and suffixes ... 34
Suffixes –ant, –ent, –ance, –ence, –ancy, –ency ... 36
Suffixes –cious, –tious, –cial, –tial ... 38

Unit 4: Vocabulary ... 40
Figurative language ... 40
Year 5 word list ... 42
Thematic language ... 44
Topic words ... 46

Unit 5: Reading comprehension 1 ... 48
Five Children and It, by E. Nesbit ... 48
Mary Anning, by Robert Snedden ... 52
Lord Neptune, by Judith Nicholls ... 56

Unit 6: Reading comprehension 2 ... 58
Walk Two Moons, by Sharon Creech ... 58
I Am Malala, by Malala Yousafzai with Patricia McCormick ... 62
Jia-Wen's Grandad, by Matt Goodfellow ... 66

Unit 7: Reading comprehension 3 ... 68
The House with Chicken Legs, by Sophie Anderson ... 68
Magic of Jinn, by Stephen Krensky and Giles Clare ... 72
Medusa and Minotaur Take Tea, by Rachel Piercey ... 76

Writing skills: My Mythical Relative ... 80

Final practice ... 82

Subjects, verbs and objects

Remember

Every sentence contains a subject and a verb. The subject 'does' the verb. For example: '**The cat** eats'. Sentences may contain an object which has the verb 'done' to it. For example: 'The cat eats **fish**'. The subject must agree with the verb. '**The cat eats** fish'.

Practise

1. Circle the subject in each sentence. Underline the object in each sentence that has one.

   a. (Mia) likes <u>horses</u> a lot.

   b. My (grandad) gave his collection of <u>medals</u> to me for my birthday.

   c. The exhausted (builder) drank a huge glass of <u>water</u>.

   d. My annoying (dog) <u>barks</u> constantly.

2. Tick to show whether the subject and the verb agree.

Sentence	Subject and verb agree	Subject and verb do not agree
a. The young doctor were late for work.		
b. Some people believe in aliens.		
c. Why aren't she allowed to play later?		

▷ Extend

3. Circle the subject, underline the verb and put a box around the object in each sentence. One has been done for you.

   a. (They) <u>enjoyed</u> [the giant iced buns].

   b. We saw them last week in the park.

   c. His cousin grabbed him by the back of his shirt just in time.

   d. More and more people read the news online these days.

4) Circle the correct verb in each sentence so that the subject and verb agree.

   a. Ranvir and Vicki **fetches / fetch** some toys from under the stairs.

   b. Don't / Doesn't he remind you of someone?

   c. All children in Year 5 **was / were** invited to the school disco.

   d. Some oil **is / are** leaking all over the floor!

Apply

5) Write a sentence including:

   a. a subject, a verb, and an object.

   _____

   b. a subject and a verb, but no object.

   _____

   c. a pronoun used as a subject, a verb and a pronoun used as an object.

   _____

6) Rewrite these sentences so that the verbs agree with the subject.

   a. The young singer are upset because she have lost her voice.

   _____

   b. Wasn't we supposed to leave this morning?

   _____

   c. The football team were heading to the ground for practice.

   _____

   d. "Everybody know that the moon is made of cheese," he say.

   _____

Relative clauses

> **Remember**
>
> Relative clauses add information about the noun or noun phrase in a sentence. They are a type of subordinate clause that is related to the noun. They begin with a relative pronoun such as 'who', 'whose', 'that' or 'which'. For example: 'My friend, **who** is from Liverpool, loves playing football'.

Practise

1 Underline the relative clause in each sentence.

    a. My sister lives in Bude, which is a seaside town in Cornwall.

    b. Logan, whose spelling test scores are excellent, reads a dictionary at bedtime.

    c. I'm scared of the dog that barked at me.

    d. The stew, which was steaming and aromatic, made his mouth water.

    e. Isn't that the man who set the world record for eating sausages?

2 The sentences in **Question 1** use **four** different relative pronouns to introduce the relative clauses. Write the **four** relative pronouns used.

_____

Extend

3 Write the correct relative pronoun to complete each sentence.

    a. The old pop song, _____ was my dad's favourite, blasted from the speakers.

    b. The doorbell woke up the baby, _____ had been sound asleep.

    c. Toby, _____ grandma makes amazing brownies, organised a cake sale for charity.

    d. The danger was caused by a hot-air balloon _____ had drifted off course.

4 Write the noun that each relative clause is related to in **Question 3**.

a. _____

b. _____

c. _____

d. _____

Apply

5 Write a relative clause of your own to complete each sentence. Start with the relative pronoun shown.

a. The new player, **who** _____,

scored a fantastic goal.

b. Polar bears can be found near the North Pole, **which** _____

_____.

c. My cousin Kelsey, **whose** _____,

is almost ten.

d. The biscuits **that** _____

are made using a secret recipe.

6 Write **three** sentences of your own containing relative clauses.

a. _____
_____

b. _____
_____

c. _____
_____

Tip Begin the relative clause with a relative pronoun ('who', 'whose', 'that' or 'which').

Modal verbs

Remember

A modal verb is used before another verb to change its meaning. Some modal verbs show how possible or necessary something is. For example: 'I **might** go to the cinema today'. They can be used in questions and in negative forms. For example: 'should' would become 'should**n't**' in the negative form.

Practise

1 **a.** Circle the **10** modal verbs in the cloud.

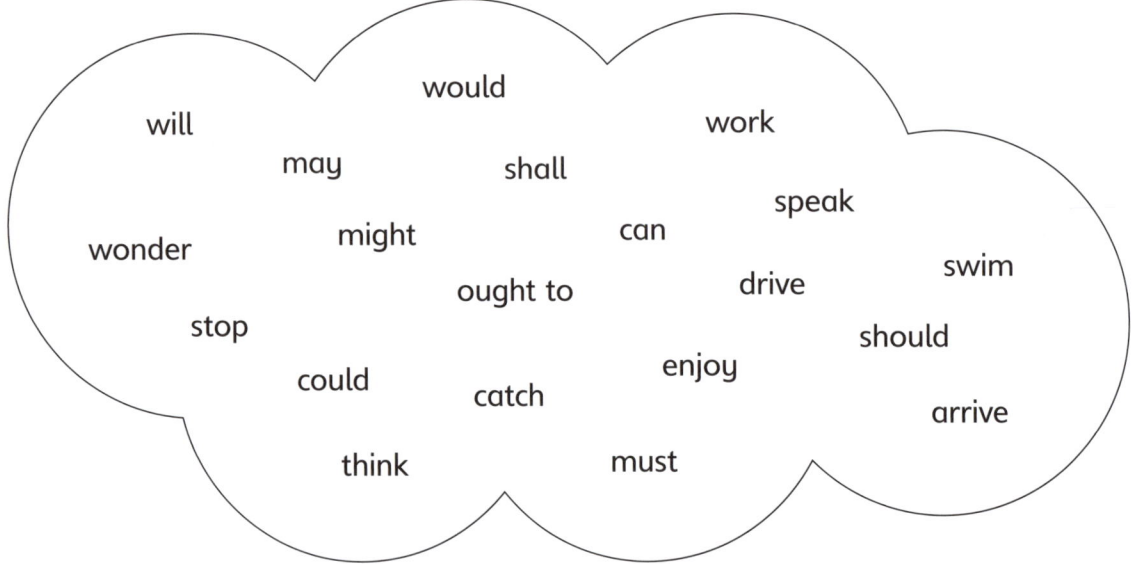

b. Choose **six** modal verbs from the cloud and write them in their negative form. One has been done for you.

shouldn't _____ _____

_____ _____ _____

Extend

2 Circle the correct modal verb in each sentence.

a. I can come over tomorrow if you **can / won't / would** like some help.

b. If we leave before dark, we **must / should / couldn't** make it home on time.

c. How **ought to / will / won't** you get to the shops next week?

8   Unit 1 • Grammar   Schofield & Sims

Apply

3) Write a sentence for each clue using a modal verb. Complete the crossword using the modal verb from your answer. One has been done for you.

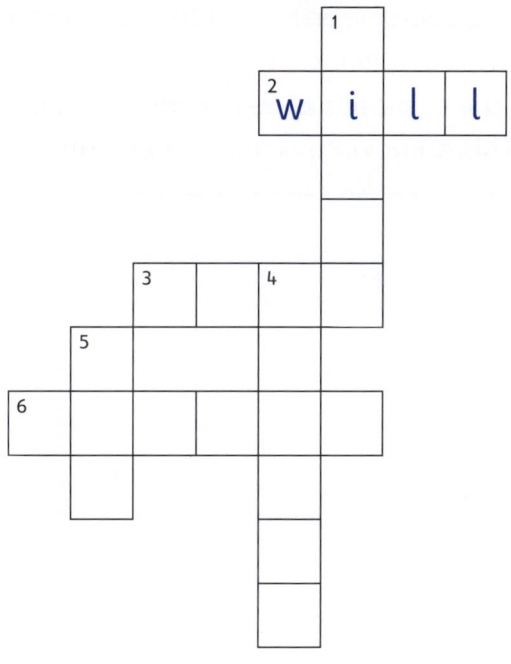

Across

2. Accept an invitation to a birthday party. (4 letters)

   <u>I will be coming to your party next week.</u>

3. Tell someone that they have to wear school uniform. (4 letters)

   _____

6. Explain that your grandma is not able to swim. (6 letters)

   _____

Down

1. Tell someone it is possible there will be a snowstorm. (5 letters)

   _____

4. Advise someone to get fit by doing a sport. (6 letters)

   _____

5. Ask very politely if you are allowed to do something. (3 letters)

   _____

Adverbials

Remember

An adverbial is a word or group of words used to describe when (adverbial of time), where (adverbial of place) or how (adverbial of manner) something is happening. For example: 'later', 'in the garden', 'in a bad mood'. Using adverbials is a good way to link ideas within and across paragraphs. This is known as cohesion in writing.

 Practise

(1) Draw lines to match each adverbial to its type.

under the floorboards	adverbial of time
full of nerves	adverbial of place
over the summer	adverbial of manner

(2) Underline the adverbial in each sentence. There may be more than one.

a. We flew to Italy and travelled by train.

b. After dinner, Alice decided to walk around the village.

c. At Christmas, Heather receives her presents with excitement.

 Extend

(3) Complete this sentence using the adverbials in the box. Use the text given in brackets to work out the type of adverbial needed.

| without a sound   at dusk   on the horizon |

_____ (time), Rick looked out to sea as storm clouds

bubbled up _____ (place) and lightning flashed

_____ (manner).

4 Write an adverbial of your own to complete each sentence.

a. Isaac was sure he had left his bag _____.

b. "Who made this mess?" he demanded, _____.

c. We may even see cars flying around _____.

d. _____, a beautiful princess lived in an enormous palace by the sea.

Apply

5 Complete this story using the adverbials in the box. Use each adverbial once.

with a smile on her face	without warning	last autumn	secondly
behind her	in a grump	the very first morning
every day	in a fit of giggles	in the countryside	from head to toe

_____, Mum told me that we were going on holiday _____.

"But you'll make me go on a walk _____!" I moaned.

"Firstly, it's a beautiful place," Mum replied. "_____, all that fresh air will be good for you."

"I like ugly places and indoor air," I said _____.

_____, Mum forced me to lace up my boots. I trudged _____ along the lane.

"Come on, Eliza," Mum said, striding ahead _____.

"Isn't it wonderful?"

_____, a tractor rumbled past. One of its giant knobbly tyres squelched through a large puddle on the road. A sheet of brown water sprayed out, covering Mum _____. Dripping wet, Mum stood still in shock. I almost collapsed _____.

Cohesion in writing

Remember

'Cohesion' means making sentences and paragraphs link together well. Conjunctions (such as 'then', 'because', 'when') and adverbials (such as 'after that', 'at that moment') can be used as cohesive devices.

Cohesive devices can have different functions. For example: 'firstly' might be used to sequence ideas across paragraphs and 'while' might introduce a contrast.

Practise

1. Circle the words that create cohesion in these sentences.

   a. Noah ate a huge cream bun, so he didn't want his dinner later.

   b. We just got back from our holiday. It was great except for one thing.

   c. It will rain this morning, but later the skies will clear.

   d. I am vegetarian. Likewise, my sister tries to avoid eating meat.

   e. Freya was nervous. At lunchtime, she would perform in her first concert.

   f. Many adverbs end in the suffix –ly. For example: 'happily', 'slowly' and 'consequently'.

2. Write the correct cohesive device to complete each sentence. Use each word once.

   | however | eventually | overall | nevertheless |

   a. The rocket launch was a success. _____, the rover crashed on landing.

   b. Seren's workshop looked better. _____, she felt she had done a good job of tidying up.

   c. Jakub had been waiting for ages. _____, he gave up and went home.

   d. I didn't practise my spelling this week. _____, I got full marks in the test!

Extend

3) Sort these words into the table according to their function as a cohesive device. Three have been done for you.

~~and~~   ~~equally~~   ~~next~~   for instance   furthermore   before   unlike   in addition   meanwhile   on the contrary   as shown by   however   now   although   secondly

Adding, emphasising or giving an example	Comparing or contrasting	Sequencing
and	equally	next

Apply

4) Rewrite this paragraph using conjunctions and adverbials to link the sentences and improve cohesion.

> Dad suggested we go jogging together. I wasn't sure about it. I don't like running. My legs get tired quickly. I run out of breath going uphill. He kept asking me about it. I would make an excuse. I had homework to do. I was tired after PE at school. I ran out of excuses. The day of 'The Great Jog' arrived.

The perfect forms

Remember

The present and past perfect are both verb forms of the past tense. The present perfect uses 'has/have' and the past tense form of the main verb to describe events that have been completed in the present. For example: 'They **have walked** here'. The past perfect always uses 'had' followed by the past tense form of the main verb to describe an event completed in the past. For example: 'They **had walked** for three hours'.

Practise

1 Tick to show the verb tense used in each sentence.

Sentence	Simple past	Present perfect	Past perfect
a. The dog had wolfed down his bowl of food before his nap.			
b. We have been surfing many times.			
c. Somebody knocked loudly on the door.			
d. She had read the article already.			

Extend

2 Write the verb given in brackets in the present perfect tense to complete these sentences.

a. We _____ (to lose) our luggage at some point during this long and tiring journey.

b. I _____ (to tell) you so many times how dangerous that is!

c. Minal _____ (to be) a pharmacist for six years.

d. My cousin _____ (to stop) learning how to play the trumpet because it is too loud.

e. _____ she just _____ (to buy) a new car?

f. _____ you ever _____ (to eat) sushi before?

3) Write the verb given in brackets in the past perfect tense to complete these sentences.

   a. He _____ (to meet) up with his friends before the party.

   b. By the time we got there, the train _____ already _____ (to leave).

   c. When the fire engine eventually arrived, the fire _____ (to grow) out of control.

   d. _____ the milkman _____ (to be) when you got up this morning?

Apply

4) Use your own ideas to complete these sentences. Use the present perfect tense in your answer.

   a. He is leaving in a minute, but the others _____.

   b. My aunt asked me, "_____?"

   c. Although I have never been to Wales, I _____.

   d. In the final race of the year, she _____.

   e. Finally, we _____.

5) Use your own ideas to complete these sentences. Use the past perfect tense in your answer.

   a. I tried to stop him, but he _____.

   b. The lawn was brown because _____.

   c. Before I went to France, I _____.

   d. Until last night, they _____.

   e. Fortunately, we _____.

Tip The past perfect helps to show that one event happened before another in the past.

Using tenses consistently

Remember

The same tense is used throughout a sentence when the time frame stays the same. For example: 'Megan **got** up, **ate** some toast and **went** to school' (all of the verbs in this sentence are in the simple past tense). If the time frame changes, then the tense can change in the same sentence. For example: 'Yesterday, I **played** netball after school, but today I **am going** swimming'.

Practise

1. Circle the correct verb form in each sentence so that the tenses are consistent.

    a. That evening, Ethan **drives / drove** to town and went to the cinema.

    b. She **has slipped / will slip** on the ice and has fractured her ankle.

    c. He was reading the news on his mobile phone while he **will walk / was walking** through the park.

    d. It had all happened suddenly when the water pipe in the kitchen **had burst / has burst**.

2. Write the tense used in each sentence in **Question 1**.

    present perfect   simple past   past perfect   past progressive

    a. _____

    b. _____

    c. _____

    d. _____

Tip The past progressive is sometimes called 'the past tense with –ing' because it is made using a form of 'to be' and a word ending in –ing. For example: 'I was running'.

>> Extend

3 Rewrite these sentences so that the tenses are consistent and the sentences make sense.

   a. Yesterday, we are searching for ages and located the ruined castle.
   _____

   b. The train has departed from Edinburgh but it had not reached its destination.
   _____

   c. Emma was walking in the mountains while Andy is swimming in the lake.
   _____

4 Write a clause of your own to complete each sentence. Use the same tense as in the first clause.

   a. We followed a narrow path and _____.

   b. Imogen has fallen ill and _____.

   c. She crossed the river and _____.

   d. Joshua had come over, but _____.

Apply

5 Write a clause of your own to complete each sentence. Use a different verb form to show that the time frame has changed. One has been done for you.

   a. He is enjoying the cake <u>that I baked and decorated with colourful</u>

   <u>sprinkles yesterday afternoon.</u>_____.

   b. Mum said, "Sophie has a cold, so _____

   _____."

   c. Samira bought the new console as soon as _____

   _____."

   d. The pilot said, "We have started our descent and _____

   _____."

Primary Practice English Year 5 **17**

Adverbs of possibility

> **Remember**
>
> Adverbs are used to give more information about verbs. Some adverbs, called adverbs of possibility, are used to show how certain or uncertain something is. For example: 'It will **definitely** rain this evening' or 'She will **probably** go to the party'.

Practise

1) Circle the adverbs of possibility in the cloud.

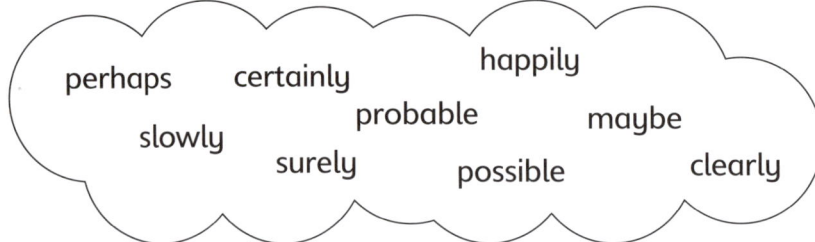

2) Write these adverbs of possibility on the line to show how uncertain or certain they suggest something is.

definitely   probably   maybe   surely

⟵────────────────────────────────⟶
uncertain   certain

Extend

3) Complete these sentences using the adverbs of possibility in the box. Use each word once.

probably   undoubtedly   potentially   perhaps

a. In the future, cars could _____ run only on water.

b. The forecast is for cold weather, meaning it will _____ snow tomorrow.

c. It is the best restaurant in town so the meal will _____ be delicious.

d. _____ I will win if we play another game.

4 Cross out the adverb of possibility in bold in each sentence. Replace it with a different adverb of possibility, using the text given in brackets to decide whether it should be more or less certain.

a. Next week, we will **definitely** _____ (less certain) visit Grandma and Grandad.

b. **Perhaps** _____ (more certain) you should apologise for what you did.

c. Peanut butter is **surely** _____ (less certain) the best spread in the world.

d. **Maybe** _____ (more certain) they are late because they missed the bus.

Apply

5 Use your own ideas to complete these sentences. Think about how certain or uncertain the adverb of possibility is.

a. I was thinking we could possibly _____.

b. I can't come over today, but maybe _____.

c. From your reaction, you clearly _____.

d. She is obviously _____.

6 Use your own ideas to write a short paragraph about something that might happen in the future. Use some adverbs of possibility to show how likely or unlikely your ideas will be.

_____
_____
_____
_____
_____

Tip Look at the adverbs of possibility in **Questions 1** to **5** for ideas.

Expanded noun phrases

Remember

Expanded noun phrases can be used to improve writing. Noun phrases such as 'the monster' can be expanded using adjectives. For example: 'the **huge, ugly** monster'. However, they can also be expanded further by adding prepositional phrases: 'the huge, ugly monster **with sharp claws**'.

Practise

1. Sort these words into the table. Decide if they are adjectives, determiners or prepositions.

| behind | an | near | over | three | in | aggressive |
| on | scary | fast | those | enormous | my | the |

Adjectives	Determiners	Prepositions

2. Label the different parts of the expanded noun phrases. Write **A** for adjective, **D** for determiner, **N** for noun and **P** for prepositional phrase.

   a. some red cars
      ↑   ↑   ↑
      __   __ __

   b. many small, pretty birds
      ↑   ↑   ↑   ↑
      __   __   __   __

   c. that old farmhouse in the countryside
      ↑   ↑   ↑   ↑
      __   __   __   __

   d. another long, hard think about the mistake
      ↑   ↑   ↑   ↑   ↑
      __   __   __   __   __

Extend

3 Write adjectives, determiners and prepositional phrases to make expanded noun phrases.

a. the _____ fish

b. lots of _____, _____ stories

c. that _____ café _____

d. _____ _____, _____ books
_____

4 Write expanded noun phrases for these words. Remember to use adjectives, determiners and prepositional phrases.

a. their cat

_____

b. dust

_____

c. river

_____

Apply

5 Use your own ideas to write part of a short story. Use expanded noun phrases to describe the characters, objects and setting. You could base your writing on real life or stories that you know.

_____
_____
_____
_____
_____

Parentheses

Remember

A parenthesis is a word, phrase or clause added to a sentence to give extra information. The parenthesis is placed between a pair of commas **, ,** or brackets **( )** or dashes **– –**. For example: Tom, **the best runner in the school**, won the race. Importantly, the sentence should still make sense if the parenthesis is removed.

Practise

1. Underline the parenthesis and its punctuation.

   a. The flight – from Rome to New York – left a few minutes late.

   b. Today was a great success (we won the final).

   c. Sammy, a long-haired guitarist from Liverpool, hitchhiked around Spain last summer.

   d. You can believe me – no, don't laugh – because I'm telling the truth.

   e. The race (the first of the day) started at 9 o'clock sharp.

   f. My best friend Rima, who lives a few doors down, bought me a present.

Tip The parenthesis is the part of the sentence that gives extra information. Try reading the rest of the sentence aloud without the parenthesis to check that it still makes sense.

2. Tick the sentences where a parenthesis has been used.

The well-behaved children (all five of them) got a reward from the teacher. ☐

She ran to catch the train, but she was too late. ☐

How far – more or less – would you say it is to Land's End? ☐

The shopping centre, which opened last year, is a great place to visit. ☐

The strange banging noise was just the back gate in the wind – or was it? ☐

On holiday, Dad slipped and fell into the pool (it was the funniest thing ever!). ☐

Extend

3 Tick **two** to show where the punctuation should go to make a parenthesis in each sentence.

a. He is the person some people claim who carried out the robbery. (brackets)
☐ ☐ ☐ ☐

b. My Uncle Louis a fun-loving, cheerful man decided to write a sitcom for TV. (commas)
☐ ☐ ☐ ☐

c. The players all eleven of them celebrated with the fans on the pitch. (dashes)
☐ ☐ ☐ ☐

4 Rewrite these sentences using the type of punctuation in brackets to create parentheses.

a. That man over there the one in the blue jacket wants to speak to you. (commas)

_____

b. The wait and it had felt like forever! was finally over. (dashes)

_____

c. Lacey forgot her PE kit again she really should know the day by now. (brackets)

_____

Apply

5 Write a parenthesis of your own to complete these sentences.

a. The winners (_____)

will collect their prize on Friday.

b. That is Hannah, _____,

sitting over there.

c. I read her book – _____

– in one sitting.

Primary Practice **English Year 5**   23

Commas for clarity

Remember

Commas are useful for making writing clearer and easier to read. They are used to separate single words, phrases and other parts of a sentence, such as items in a list, adjectives in an expanded noun phrase, a parenthesis, a main and subordinate clause, or a fronted adverbial. For example: commas separate adjectives in a list in the sentence 'Omar is caring, thoughtful and kind'.

Practise

1 Add commas in the correct places in these sentences, then circle the reason for the commas.

   a. Misha was young __ sensitive __ and enthusiastic.

   to separate adjectives in a list   to separate a subordinate clause

   b. Although Millie __ was late __ she still managed __ to catch her flight.

   to separate a subordinate clause   to separate adjectives in an expanded noun phrase

   c. My new Labrador puppy __ whose name is Poppy __ keeps digging holes __ in the garden.

   to separate nouns in a list   to separate a relative clause

   d. Dylan __ a talented sprinter __ from Nottingham __ has qualified __ for the next Olympics.

   to separate a parenthesis   to separate a fronted adverbial

   e. Due to the storm __ I'm afraid __ the annual school sports day __ has been cancelled.

   to separate nouns in a list   to separate a fronted adverbial

Extend

2 Circle the commas in these sentences that are in the correct place.

   a. For breakfast, I will, be having bacon, and eggs, toast, jam and fruit, juice.

   b. It was definitely, him, that, tall, noisy boy in Year 3, who pushed, over the flowerpot.

3 The commas in these sentences are in the wrong places. Rewrite the sentences, putting the commas in the correct places.

a. Whether we like it, or not Glenda my great-aunt, from Canada is coming to stay, for a month!
_____
_____

b. At midnight that new video, game which has five-star reviews will be, released.
_____
_____

Apply

4 Write a sentence of your own using a comma or commas and including:

a. a parenthesis.
_____
_____

b. a list of adjectives in an expanded noun phrase.
_____
_____

c. a fronted adverbial.
_____
_____

5 Add **10** commas in the correct places in this paragraph.

Every year tens of thousands of cyclists take part in the biggest bike race in the world. The race takes place in Cape Town South Africa every March. The cyclists all race individually unlike in the Tour de France which is a team race. There are professional cyclists keen amateurs and others riding just for fun or for charity. Around 100 kilometres long the route starts and finishes in the shadow of Table Mountain which is one of the seven natural wonders of the world. The competitors face a series of steep hills strong headwinds and speedy descents on one of the most beautiful challenging races on any continent.

Silent and unstressed letters

> **Remember**
>
> Some words contain silent letters or unstressed letters. For example: some words contain a silent 'k' or 'w', such as '**k**night' or '**w**rist'. Silent letters can be in the middle or at the end of words, for example: 'mus**c**le' or 'lam**b**'. Unstressed letters are often vowel sounds, such as in 'diff**e**rent' and 'sep**a**rate'.

Practise

1 a. Sort these words into the correct box. There should be **five** words in each box.

| formula | identity | carrots | octopus | listen |
| thumb | gnawed | knock | regulate | fright |

Words with all letters pronounced	Words with silent or unstressed letters

b. Write the **five** words with silent letters from **Question 1a**. Circle the silent letters in each word.

Extend

2 Write the missing silent letters to complete each word.

a. ___ sychic

b. Feb ___ uary

c. li ___ ___ tning

d. condem ___

e. ___ nashed

f. autum ___

Unit 3 • Spelling

3 Rewrite these words with the correct spellings.

a. genral _____   b. choclate _____

c. nuckle _____   d. sychology _____

e. probly _____   f. fasinating _____

Apply

4 Complete this crossword using the clues.

Across
2. writing, such as novels, plays and poems
5. a building where you borrow books
6. a piece of land surrounded by water
7. something that keeps your attention is …
9. a plant or root used for food

Down
1. the day before Thursday
3. the natural world in which people, animals and plants live
4. how you feel when you are relaxed
8. to be uncertain about

Homophones and near homophones

Remember

Homophones are words that sound the same but have different spellings and meanings. For example: 'boy' (a male child) and 'buoy' (a type of float). Near homophones sound similar when spoken, but not exactly the same. They also have different spellings and meanings. For example: 'accept' and 'except'.

Practise

1 Draw lines to match the homophones or near homophones.

aisle	altar
aloud	desert
draught	isle
alter	draft
dessert	allowed

Extend

2 Complete each sentence using the homophones in **Question 1**.

a. The pirates were not _____ to set foot on the _____ .

b. The vicar walked down the _____ towards the _____ .

c. After eating _____, I sat down to prepare the first _____ of my speech.

d. A cool _____ helped her sleep in her hot, stuffy tent in the _____ .

e. You may need to _____ the volume of your voice when speaking _____ .

3 Underline the correct meanings of these homophones, then circle the word class.

Homophone	Meaning	Word class
a. heard	a group of animals / perceived with the ear	noun / verb / adjective
b. herd	a group of animals / perceived with the ear	noun / verb / adjective
c. steal	a hard metal / to take without permission	noun / verb / adjective
d. steel	a hard metal / to take without permission	noun / verb / adjective

 Apply

4 This story uses lots of incorrect homophones. Rewrite it using the correct homophones.

At breakfast, our alien guessed ate his serial with a fork. I guest he was new to cutlery.

"Whose still hungry?" Mum asked. The alien burped. "I herd that," Mum scolded.

The alien, who's chin was covered in milk, burped again.

Afterwards, he lead me to his ship in the dessert, where he showed me a led box.

"Did you steel that last night?" I asked. The alien burped in agreement. I shook my head. "You really are a cereal burper, aren't you? I'm not sure we will ever altar that!"

_____

_____

_____

_____

_____

Base words

Remember

A base word has a meaning when used on its own, but its meaning can be changed when a suffix or prefix (or both) is added to it. For example: 'act' (base word); '**re**act' (prefix + base word); 'act**ion**' (base word + suffix); '**re**act**ion**' (prefix + base word + suffix).

Practise

1. Underline the base word in each of the words in the cloud. Circle any prefixes and put a box around any suffixes. One has been done for you.

   (re)payable   treatment   useless   unhelpful   fastest   disagreeable
   accessible   sailor   deformity   disowned   misheard   depart

2. Choose **six** of the base words you have underlined in **Question 1**. Add a prefix or a suffix to each to make a new word not already in the cloud. Do **not** use suffixes that alter the spelling of the base word.

   _____   _____   _____

   _____   _____   _____

Tip You could use prefixes and suffixes you already know. You could also see if any of the prefixes and suffixes in the cloud can be used with more than one word.

Extend

3. Add a prefix **or** a suffix to each of these base words to make a new word. Do **not** change the spelling of the base word.

   happy   cycle   view   break   care   norm

   _____   _____   _____

   _____   _____   _____

30 Unit 3 • Spelling   Schofield & Sims

4 Add a prefix **and** a suffix to each of these base words to make a new word. Do **not** change the spelling of the base word.

event   like   suit   place   spell   miss

_____   _____   _____

_____   _____   _____

Apply

5 Complete this crossword using the clues and the base words shown.

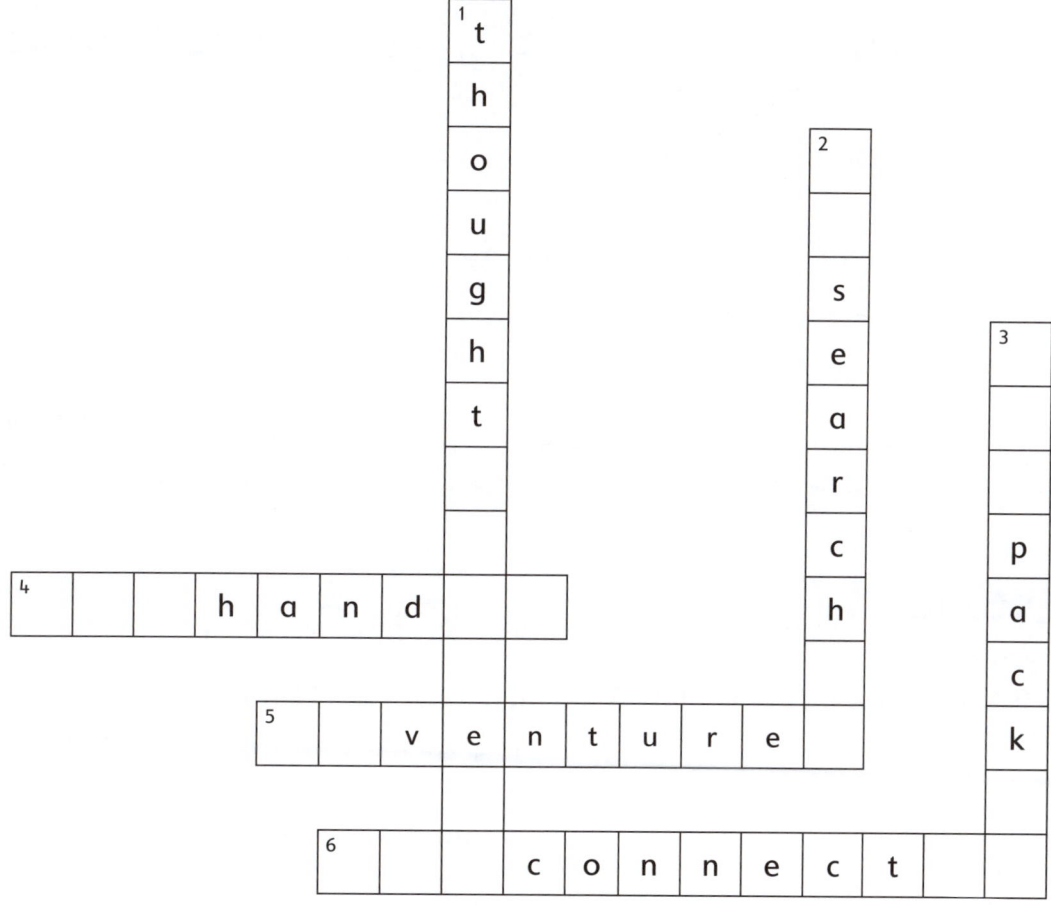

Across

4. to deal with something badly (verb)

5. someone who explores or does risky activities (noun)

6. a phone call that is cut off (adjective)

Down

1. consideration for other people (noun)

2. someone who investigates a topic (noun)

3. wrapped before being sold (adjective)

Tricky spellings

> **Remember**
>
> Some words have tricky spellings. The letter string 'ough' makes lots of different sounds. For example: bought ('aw') and bough ('ow'). The spelling rule of 'i before e' except after 'c' is used when the sound is 'ee'. For example: 'p**ie**ce' or 'dec**ei**ve'. Some words do not follow this rule and must be learnt instead.

Practise

1. Draw lines to match these words to the sound 'ough' makes. One has been done for you.

   cough   through   brought   tough   thorough   plough   although

   /uh/   /aw/   /oo/   /ow/   /off/   /uff/   /oh/

2. Circle the words in the cloud that are spelt correctly. Use a dictionary to help.

   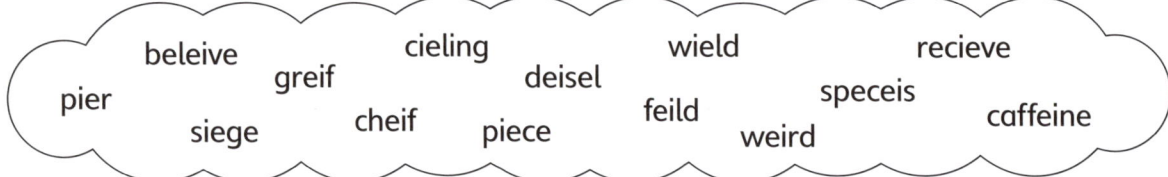

   beleive, cieling, wield, recieve, pier, greif, deisel, speceis, siege, cheif, piece, feild, weird, caffeine

Extend

3. Write the missing word in the table. They all use the 'ough' letter string. Read the word meaning and the sound the word makes to help you.

Word meaning	Sound	Word
a. a cake with a hole	/oh/	
b. not smooth	/uff/	
c. past tense of think	/aw/	
d. a water container for animals	/off/	
e. detailed or complete	/uh/	
f. a preposition meaning 'in every part'	/oo/	
g. a long period of no rain	/ow/	

Unit 3 • Spelling

4. Find the **nine** hidden words in this word search. The words run horizontally and vertically.

belief   debrief   fiendish   fierce   niece
perceive   receipts   shield   shriek

L	A	S	H	R	I	E	K	R	F
K	D	W	P	F	P	C	P	E	I
D	E	B	R	I	E	F	O	C	E
N	I	E	C	E	R	M	L	E	R
D	T	C	F	T	C	A	M	I	C
P	E	K	B	B	E	A	F	P	E
F	I	E	N	D	I	S	H	T	R
I	U	Z	R	G	V	R	X	S	C
K	B	E	L	I	E	F	E	C	U
D	W	Y	T	S	H	I	E	L	D

Apply

5. Rewrite these sentences using the correct spellings of the words.

   a. Althoh Bailey the farmer was feeling ruff, he cleaned the plow and the troff thoruhly.

   _____

   _____

   b. The theif conceived a plan to sieze his niece from the fiendish preistess.

   _____

   _____

   c. He parked his deisel car in a field nearby and retreived his toolkit from the boot.

   _____

   _____

Tip You can use a dictionary to help if needed. Think about how the word might be spelt based on the spelling patterns you know and check in the dictionary to see if you are correct.

Prefixes and suffixes

Remember

Prefixes and suffixes can change a word's meaning and word class. Adding a prefix can change a verb to a negative, opposite or different meaning. For example: 'appear' becomes '**dis**appear'.

Nouns and adjectives can become verbs when the suffixes –en, –ise, –ify or –ate are added. For example: 'light' (noun or adjective) + –en becomes 'light**en**' (verb).

Practise

1) Read the clues. Circle the verb with the correct prefix.

a.	the opposite of 'tie'	distie	detie	untie
b.	the negative of 'inform'	reinform	misinform	underinform
c.	to work too much	overwork	transwork	diswork
d.	the negative of 'agree'	deagree	disagree	misagree

2) Circle the correct form of the verb made by adding a suffix to the noun or adjective in bold.

a.	**beauty**	beauten	beautify	beautise
b.	**personal**	personalise	personalate	personalify
c.	**vaccine**	vaccinify	vaccinise	vaccinate
d.	**ripe**	ripate	ripise	ripen

Extend

3) Add the correct prefix to each word. Use each prefix once.

un	dis	trans	mis	over	fore	re	sub

a. _____ please   **b.** _____ block   **c.** _____ merge   **d.** _____ cast

e. _____ plant   **f.** _____ behave   **g.** _____ heat   **h.** _____ claim

4 Circle the word class for each word, then change the word into a verb by adding the correct suffix from the box. Use each suffix once.

> ate   en   ise   ify

a. glory (noun / adjective) _____ (verb)

b. summary (noun / adjective) _____ (verb)

c. assassin (noun / adjective) _____ (verb)

d. sad (noun / adjective) _____ (verb)

Apply

5 Write **two** sentences using any verbs that can be made using these prefixes.

> de   inter   be   pre   co   out   under

a. _____

_____

b. _____

_____

6 Write the verb forms of the words given in brackets to complete the paragraph.

The police have not _____ (identity) a suspect yet. The owner of the

flower shop was _____ (critic) because he had not

_____ (active) the security camera. During the break-in, someone

completely _____ (flat) the flowers.

"It was _____ (fright) and it will take ages to

_____ (straight) out," said the owner.

The police replied, "We _____ (real) this is a worrying time and we will

_____ (intense) our investigation."

Suffixes –ant, –ent, –ance, –ence, –ancy, –ency

Remember

The suffix –ant is often used to form adjectives linked to a noun ending –ation. For example: 'hesit**ation**' becomes 'hesit**ant**'. The suffixes –ance and –ancy are noun endings. For example: 'hesit**ancy**'. The suffixes –ent, –ence or –ency are often used when the letter before is a soft 'c', 'g' or 'qu'. For example: 'inno**c**ent', 'emer**g**ency' or 'conse**qu**ence'.

Practise

1. Complete the table by changing the suffix of each noun. One has been done for you.

Noun	Adjective	Noun (–ance or –ancy)
a. observation	observant	observance
b. radiation		
c. vacation		
d. consultation		

2. Circle the correct spelling in each sentence.

a. The man explained the **urgency** / **urgancy** of the situation to me.

b. The family made **frequant** / **frequent** trips to the Lake District.

c. Stephan was convinced that he would become a secret **agent** / **agant**.

d. As children grow older, they often want greater **independance** / **independence**.

Extend

3. Complete each word by adding an appropriate –ant, –ance or –ancy suffix so that the sentence makes sense.

a. Ella understood the import_____ of trying her best.

b. The detective reported that the new clue was signific_____.

c. Aisha's parents were delighted about her aunt's pregn_____.

d. The brilli_____ of the neon signs in Tokyo brings the city alive.

4 Complete each word by adding an appropriate –ent, –ence or –ency suffix so that the sentence makes sense.

   a. The woman did not even have the dec_____ to apologise for knocking me over.

   b. It was such a coincid_____ that we bumped into our friends on holiday.

   c. A transluc_____ material lets some light through; a transpar_____ material lets lots of light through.

   d. Our puppy has a tend_____ to run off and hide in the park.

Apply

5 Rewrite these sentences using the correct spellings.

   a. I improved my fluancy in French so I could ask for some currancy at the bank.
   _____

   b. There was silance as the judge pronounced the defendent innocent.
   _____

   c. The adolescant studant was confidant when she gave her presentation.
   _____

6 Write **three** sentences using your choice of these –ant, –ance and –ancy words.

| tolerant | infancy | attendance | vibrancy | disturbance |
| assistance | applicant | ignorance | reluctant | buoyancy |

   a. _____
   _____

   b. _____
   _____

   c. _____
   _____

Primary Practice **English Year 5**

Suffixes –cious, –tious, –cial, –tial

Remember

The suffixes –cious, –tious, –cial and –tial can all be used to make adjectives. Usually, –cious is used if the root word ends in 'ce' and –tious if it ends in 'tion'. For example: 'gra**ce**' becomes 'gra**cious**'; 'ambi**tion**' becomes 'ambi**tious**'. The suffix –cial is used after a vowel and –tial is used after a consonant. For example: 'off**ice**' becomes 'off**icial**'; 'esse**nce**' becomes 'esse**ntial**'.

Practise

1) Change these root words into adjectives using the suffixes –cial or –tial.

a. benefit _____   b. substance _____

c. sacrifice _____   d. president _____

e. confidence _____   f. artifice _____

2) Circle the adjectives with the correct –cious and –tious suffixes in the cloud.

delitious   fictitious   suspitious
vicious   caucious   precious   conscious
infecious   atrotious   luscious

Extend

3) The words in these sentences do **not** follow the rules you know. Circle the correct spelling in each sentence. Use a dictionary to help.

a. I went to the bank to ask for some **finantial / financial** advice.

b. When she saw what had happened, her **initial / inicial** reaction was complete shock.

c. In some countries, TV adverts are called **commercials / commertials**.

d. The match was ruined by a **controvertial / controversial** decision.

4 Change these nouns to adjectives using the suffixes –cious or –tious.

a. nutrition _____   b. ferocity _____

c. malice _____   d. space _____

e. caution _____   f. pretention _____

Apply

5 Rewrite this paragraph using the correct spellings. There are **eight** incorrect spellings in total.

> Yesterday was a spetial day. We were moving to a residencial area in a provintial location. The new house was not palacial, but it had potencial. The building needed some substancial and essencial repairs. Unfortunately, on the first night, there was a storm and the rain was torrencial.

_____

_____

_____

_____

6 Add the suffix –cious or –tious to **three** of these nouns. Write **three** sentences using the –cious or –tious adjectives you have made.

> fiction   suspicion   infection   superstition   audacity

a. _____

_____

b. _____

_____

c. _____

_____

Figurative language

> **Remember**
>
> Figurative language is mostly used in fiction and poetry to create images for the reader. Hyperbole creates exaggeration to emphasise meaning or add humour or drama. Imagery uses the senses (sound, sight, smell, taste and touch) to create a vivid picture or feeling.

Practise

1) Tick to show which sentences contain hyperbole.

His smile was a mile wide. ☐

The pictures in the book were colourful and detailed. ☐

This homework is going to take me forever. ☐

Cassie wondered if the wolf outside would eventually leave. ☐

2) Write the type of sense used in each sentence to create imagery.

a. The powerful aroma of roses filled the night air. _____

b. The skin on her palms felt as rough as sandpaper. _____

c. I fancy a warm, buttery scone with thick, sweet jam and cream. _____

d. The setting sun is a burnt orange saucer balanced on the horizon. _____

e. The thundering of a thousand hooves rumbled through the valley. _____

Extend

3) Complete each sentence using hyperbole.

a. I'm so hungry I could _____!

b. He's as thin _____.

c. I've seen this film _____.

d. She can run as fast _____.

4 Complete these sentences using the type of imagery given in brackets.

  a. Her perfume _____. (smell)

  b. That drink _____. (taste)

  c. My hair _____. (touch)

  d. The firework _____. (sound)

  e. The sea _____. (sight)

Apply

5 Write a description of a made-up monster who lives under your bed. Use hyperbole and imagery in your answer. The first sentence has been done for you.

Under my bed, my monster's snores are like rolling thunder.

_____
_____
_____
_____
_____
_____
_____
_____
_____
_____

Tip Remember to think about the different senses when writing your description.

Year 5 word list

Remember

There is a list of words to learn in Years 5 and 6. The Year 5 word list includes a range of different word classes, such as nouns, adjectives, verbs and adverbs. Use these activities to practise some of the words.

Practise

1) Write each word from the box, then draw lines to match each word to its word class and meaning. One has been done for you.

> ~~profession~~   occupy   conscious   rhythm   mischievous

profession   adjective   fond of causing trouble

_____   adjective   a repeated pattern of sounds

_____   verb   to live in

_____   noun   awake and aware

_____   noun   a paid job requiring special training

2) Choose a word from the box to complete each sentence, then write its word class in the brackets. Use each word once.

> frequently   twelfth   government   appreciate

a. This must be the _____ time you have lost your keys!

(_____)

b. On Thursday, people will vote for a new _____ in the election.

(_____)

c. My mother and my aunt speak _____ on the phone.

(_____)

d. _____ the things you have, not the things you think you want.

(_____)

Extend

3 **a.** Write the missing letters for each adjective, then draw lines to match it to its meaning.

av __ r __ ge   full of purpose and persistence

d __ term __ ned   enough or adequate

suf __ __ c __ ent   ordinary or usual

b. Write the missing letters for each noun, then draw lines to match it to its meaning.

lang __ __ ge   a strong interest in understanding

enviro __ __ ent   a system of words for communicating

cur __ __ sity   the natural world

Apply

4 Read the words in this table. If you do not know what they mean, use a dictionary to look them up.

Nouns	Adjectives	Verbs	Adverbs
dictionary, equipment, lightning, muscle, secretary, shoulder, soldier, stomach, symbol, system, temperature, yacht	ancient, apparent, attached, definite, excellent, forty, relevant	achieve, communicate, criticise, develop, exaggerate, occur, recognise, recommend, rhyme, suggest	especially, immediately

a. Write a sentence that uses **two** nouns from the table.

_____

b. Write a sentence that uses **one** noun and **one** adverb from the table.

_____

c. Write a sentence that uses **one** noun, **one** adjective and **one** verb from the table.

_____

_____

Primary Practice **English Year 5**

Thematic language

> **Remember**
>
> The words on these pages link to the themes explored in the reading comprehension units. A dictionary and thesaurus can be useful to look up the meaning of the words and find synonyms and antonyms. Widening knowledge of vocabulary helps to improve spoken language, reading and writing.

Practise

1 a. Sort the following words into the table, then use a dictionary to check the meaning of each word.

> scour   ditty   petty   anchor   honour
>
> imitate   quarry   ungainly   occupation

Words with meanings I know	Words with meanings I can guess	Words with meanings I don't know

b. Choose **one** word from the table with a meaning you did not know. Write a sentence using the word to show that you now understand what it means.

_____

_____

Extend

2 Circle the word that is closest in meaning to the word in bold.

a. specific	normal	only	particular
b. chime	ring	fizzle	click
c. malice	dirt	hatred	kindness
d. identical	opposite	distinct	interchangeable
e. linger	grasp	wait	abandon

Tip Try reading the words in bold aloud in a sentence, then replace them with the other options to check which word has a similar meaning.

3 Write the missing letters for each word using the meaning given in brackets as a clue.

a. sib __ __ __ g   (a brother or sister)

b. __ nce __ t __ r   (a family relation from the past)

c. sup __ __ na __ __ __ al (cannot be explained by science)

d. __ __ rb __ __ den   (not allowed)

Apply

4 Complete these sentences using the words in the box. Use each word once.

> disgrace   replenish   extensively   infested   reputation   lopsided

a. The failed knight was forced to leave the kingdom in _____ and with his _____ in tatters.

b. When the kitchen was _____ with mice, the cooks were forced to _____ their stores with fresh food.

c. The _____ roof of the house was _____ strengthened after it nearly collapsed.

Primary Practice **English Year 5**   45

Topic words

> **Remember**
>
> The vocabulary activities on these pages are linked to interesting topics across all subjects in the curriculum. Think about prefixes, suffixes and root words when working out the meanings of these words. A dictionary and thesaurus can be useful when coming across new words for the first time.

Practise

1. Sort the words into the subjects that they would most likely be used in.

> anatomy   tundra   ramparts   genetic   doubloon   chromosome
> court   weathered   portrait   opossum   oasis   marine

Science	History	Geography

Extend

2. Circle the word that is closest in meaning to the word in bold.

a. **pail**	light	bucket	inferior
b. **carcass**	vehicle	luggage	remains
c. **associate**	connect	avoid	compare
d. **blueprint**	tactic	conspiracy	masterplan
e. **unearth**	conceal	discover	release

46   Unit 4 • Vocabulary   Schofield & Sims

3 Write the missing letters for each word using the meaning given in brackets as a clue.

a. c __ vil __ sa __ __ __ __ (a human way of life in a particular area)

b. d __ c __ y (to rot)

c. h __ __ t __ __ r (a low bush with small purple flowers)

d. __ o __ i __ o __ (the line where the earth's surface and sky meet)

Apply

4 Complete these sentences using the words in the box. Use each word once.

| discoveries | reptile | recognised | stash | diagram | crocodile |
| turret | bleak | intrepid | skeleton | distance | |

a. The _____ explorer used the _____ of the castle to locate the _____ of treasure the smugglers had hidden in the _____.

b. He made further _____ on the _____ moorland a short _____ from the castle.

c. These included the _____ of a large _____ he _____ as that of a _____.

5 Write **four** sentences of your own using some of the words in the box. You may add suffixes to the words.

| difference | fossil | desert | distance | sibling | seethe |

a. _____

b. _____

c. _____

d. _____

Five Children and It, by E. Nesbit

> This extract is from a much-loved classic story written by Edith Nesbit in 1902. Five brothers and sisters have moved to a house in the country. One day, while their parents are away, they go digging in some local gravel-pits and make a surprising discovery.

So they went. Of course they had been to the edge of the gravel-pit and looked over, but they had not gone down into it for fear Father should say they mustn't play there, and the same with the chalk-quarry. The gravel-pit is not really dangerous if you don't try to climb down the edges, but go the slow safe way round by the road, as if you were a cart.

Each of the children carried its own spade, and took it in turns to carry the Lamb. He was the baby, and they called him that because 'Baa' was the first thing he ever said. They called Anthea 'Panther', which seems silly when you read it, but when you say it it sounds a little like her name.

The gravel-pit is very large and wide, with grass growing round the edges at the top, and dry stringy wildflowers, purple and yellow. It is like a giant's wash-hand basin. […]

The children built a castle, of course, but castle-building is rather poor fun when you have no hope of the swishing tide ever coming in to fill up the moat and wash away the drawbridge, and, at the happy last, to wet everybody up to the waist at least.

Cyril wanted to dig out a cave to play smugglers in, but the others thought it might bury them alive, so it ended in all spades going to work to dig a hole through the castle to Australia. These children, you see, believed that the world was round, and that on the other side the little Australian boys and girls were really walking wrong way up, like flies on the ceiling, with their heads hanging down into the air.

The children dug and they dug and they dug, and their hands got sandy and hot and red, and their faces got damp and shiny. The Lamb had tried to eat the sand, and had cried so hard when he found that it was not, as he had supposed, brown sugar, that he was now tired out, and was lying asleep in a warm fat bunch in the middle of the half-finished castle. This left his brothers and sisters free to work really hard, and the hole that was to come out in Australia soon grew so deep that Jane, who was called Pussy for short, begged the others to stop.

"Suppose the bottom of the hole gave way suddenly," she said, "and you tumbled out among the little Australians, all the sand would get in their eyes."

"Yes," said Robert, "and they would hate us, and throw stones at us, and not let us see the kangaroos, or opossums, or bluegums, or Emu Brand birds, or anything."

Cyril and Anthea knew that Australia was not quite so near as all that, but they agreed to stop using the spades and go on with their hands. This was quite easy, because the sand at the bottom of the hole was very soft and fine and dry, like sea-sand. And there were little shells in it.

"Fancy it having been wet sea here once, all sloppy and shiny," said Jane, "with fishes and conger-eels and coral and mermaids."

"And masts of ships and wrecked Spanish treasure. I wish we could find a gold doubloon, or something," Cyril said.

"How did the sea get carried away?" Robert asked.

"Not in a pail, silly," said his brother. "Father says the earth got too hot underneath, like you do in bed sometimes, so it just hunched up its shoulders, and the sea had to slip off, like the blankets do off us, and the shoulder was left sticking out, and turned into dry land. Let's go and look for shells; I think that little cave looks likely, and I see something sticking out there like a bit of wrecked ship's anchor, and it's beastly hot in the Australian hole."

The others agreed, but Anthea went on digging. She always liked to finish a thing when she had once begun it. She felt it would be a disgrace to leave that hole without getting through to Australia.

The cave was disappointing, because there were no shells, and the wrecked ship's anchor turned out to be only the broken end of a pickaxe handle, and the cave party were just making up their minds that the sand makes you thirstier when it is not by the seaside, and someone had suggested going home for lemonade, when Anthea suddenly screamed:

"Cyril! Come here! Oh, come quick! It's alive! It'll get away! Quick!"

They all hurried back.

"It's a rat, I shouldn't wonder," said Robert. "Father says they infest old places – and this must be pretty old if the sea was here thousands of years ago."

"Perhaps it is a snake," said Jane, shuddering.

"Let's look," said Cyril, jumping into the hole. "I'm not afraid of snakes. I like them. If it is a snake I'll tame it, and it will follow me everywhere, and I'll let it sleep round my neck at night."

"No, you won't," said Robert firmly. He shared Cyril's bedroom. "But you may if it's a rat."

"Oh, don't be silly!" said Anthea, "it's not a rat, it's MUCH bigger. And it's not a snake. It's got feet; I saw them; and fur! No – not the spade. You'll hurt it! Dig with your hands."

"And let IT hurt ME instead! That's so likely, isn't it?" said Cyril, seizing a spade.

"Oh, don't!" said Anthea. "Squirrel, DON'T. I – it sounds silly, but it said something. It really and truly did."

"What?"

"It said, 'You let me alone'."

Five Children and It, by E. Nesbit

1. Look at the paragraph beginning *The gravel-pit is very large …* . What simile does the author use to describe the gravel-pit?

_____

2. Why did the baby eat some sand?

_____

3. *"And masts of ships and wrecked Spanish treasure. I wish we could find a gold doubloon, or something," Cyril said.*

Which word is closest in meaning to the word 'doubloon'? Tick **one**.

jacket ☐   coin ☐

crown ☐   medal ☐

4. How do the children know that the gravel-pit used to be by the sea? Give **two** examples.

a. _____

b. _____

5. a. Look at the paragraph beginning *The others agreed, but …*. Which of these words best describes Anthea's personality? Circle **one**.

independent   selfish   foolish   determined

b. Explain why using evidence from the text.

_____

_____

6. Does Robert prefer snakes or rats? Explain your answer using evidence from the text.

_____

_____

7 What is unusual about the creature in the hole?

_____

8 *"It said, 'You let me alone'."*

Which sentence is closest in meaning to the creature's words? Tick **one**.

Why did you leave me alone? ☐

Leave me alone. ☐

You left me alone. ☐

Let me be lonely. ☐

9 Draw lines to match each child to their nickname.

Anthea		Squirrel
Jane		Lamb
Cyril		Pussy
The baby		Panther

10 Who do you think is the leader out of the five children? Explain your answer using evidence from the text.

_____

_____

_____

Grammar in Action

Jane uses an adverb of possibility when speaking (see page 18 for adverbs of possibility).

What is the word she uses? _____

Mary Anning, by Robert Snedden

The Natural History Museum has called Mary Anning the greatest fossil hunter ever known. She discovered fossils – plants and creatures preserved in rock for millions of years – that have changed our understanding of the natural world. Her achievements inspired many scientists and paved the way for the development of geology as a science.

When Anning lived, around two centuries ago, people were beginning to rethink their ideas about how the world had come to be the way it is, and there was growing interest in geology: the science of Earth. Geologists look at the materials that Earth is made of and how they are formed. These scientists are interested in the history of our planet, and they study the processes that have shaped the land around us.

Anning's discoveries attracted attention from all over the world, yet because of the time in which she lived, Mary did not get the respect she deserved or the recognition for her achievements that she should have received. She was a working-class woman in an age when power and influence seemed to belong entirely to rich men. In spite of this, she persisted with her determination to learn all she could about the fossils she found.

Mary Anning never trained as a scientist. In fact, she only learned to read and write through lessons at her church's Sunday school. However, as she grew, she devoured articles from science journals, and her knowledge of fossils soon outstripped that of many of the successful scientists who came to examine her many outstanding discoveries.

Mary Anning was born on 21 May 1799, in the town of Lyme Regis, on the south coast of England. Her parents were Richard and Mary Anning. Childhood diseases, such as measles, were common at the time and often fatal. Of the Annings' ten children, only Mary and her older brother Joseph survived into adulthood.

Living close to the sea was also a danger. The family's home was built on a bridge and sometimes flooded in bad weather. On one occasion, the family had to crawl out of an upstairs window to avoid drowning.

Mary was only a year old when she had an extraordinarily close escape from death. On 19 August 1800, her nurse Elizabeth Haskin had taken Mary out for the day. A sudden storm sent Elizabeth running for the shelter of some elm trees. There, a flash of lightning left Elizabeth and two other women dead. By some miracle, Mary was found alive and returned unharmed to her relieved mother. According to local legend, it was the lightning that made Mary such a bright and lively child.

Mary's father, Richard Anning, was a carpenter and cabinetmaker. Once, he had the chance to repair a box for the famous writer Jane Austen during one of her visits to the town. She asked him if he could mend the box's broken lid but turned him down because his price was too high.

To earn extra money, Richard sold his fossil finds. He was an avid fossil hunter and happily shared his knowledge with his son and daughter. When they were old enough, he took Mary and her brother Joseph out along the coast to look for fossils. He made Mary a hammer with which she could extract fossils from the rocks, and he taught her how to clean them carefully. In Mary Anning's time, Lyme Regis was already a popular place for tourists, and the family added to their modest income by selling these 'curiosities' to summer visitors.

Mary Anning's formal education had been limited, but this did not stop her from reading as much scientific literature as she could lay her hands on. For Anning, hunting for fossils was not just a way of earning a living. It opened up a whole world of learning for her.

She taught herself geology, palaeontology, anatomy and scientific illustration. She would often copy scientific papers by hand, even making copies of detailed technical drawings, which were so accurate that it was hard to tell her drawings apart from the originals.

Many of the people Mary was dealing with were well-educated men of science. Her surviving letters are proof that she could share ideas with them with great confidence. Many of the scientists were impressed by her knowledge of anatomy, and she was not afraid to argue with them if she thought their ideas were mistaken. There were others, though, who refused to believe that an uneducated young woman like Anning could have such knowledge and skill.

In recent years, Anning's contribution has been more fully acknowledged in the scientific world. Scientist Stephen Jay Gould, writing in 1992, said that Anning was "probably the most important unsung collecting force in the history of palaeontology". In 2010, she was recognised by the British Royal Society as one of the ten most influential women scientists in British history.

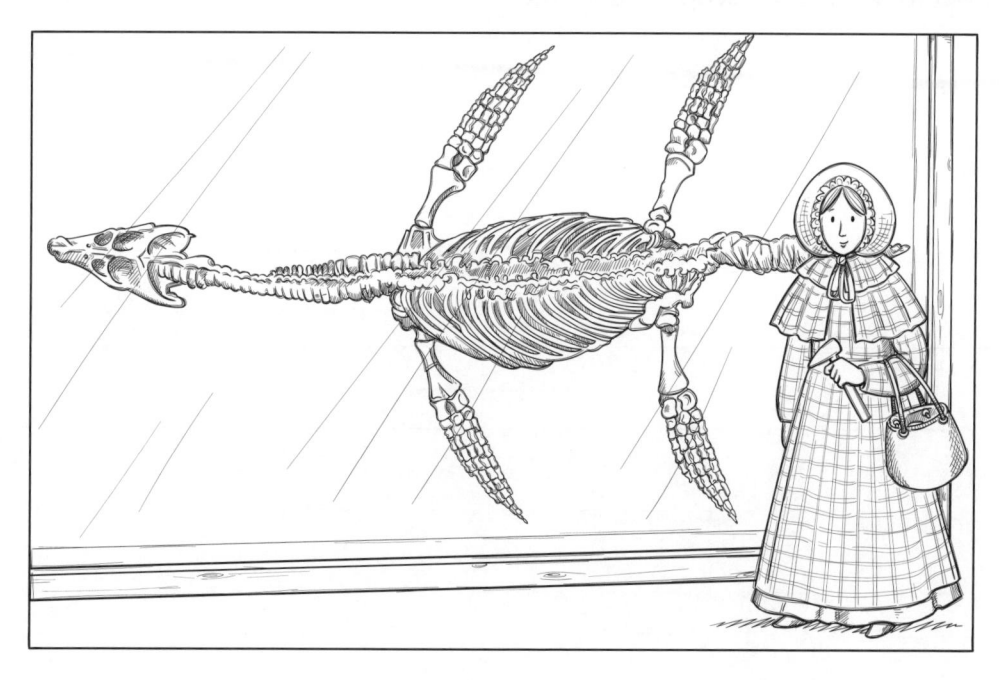

Mary Anning, by Robert Snedden

1 What are fossils?

_____

_____

2 Look at the third paragraph. Where did Mary Anning learn to read and write?

_____

3 How else did Mary Anning educate herself? Give **two** ways using evidence from the text.

_____

_____

_____

_____

4 Read the fourth and fifth paragraphs. Explain exactly where the Anning family's house was located.

_____

_____

5 Name **two** things Mary escaped as a child.

a. _____

b. _____

6 How did the Anning family make money? Give **two** examples.

_____

_____

_____

_____

7 Mary's father, Richard, is described as 'an avid fossil hunter'. Which word is closest in meaning to 'avid'? Tick **one**.

frantic ☐

irritable ☐

enthusiastic ☐

laid-back ☐

8 Why do you think fossils were called 'curiosities'?

_____

_____

9 Why did some people not recognise Mary Anning's achievements during her lifetime? Explain your answer using evidence from the text.

_____

_____

_____

_____

10 How is Mary Anning viewed now? Explain your answer using evidence from the text.

_____

_____

_____

_____

Grammar in Action

Look at the second paragraph. Find and copy an adverbial that works as a cohesive device (see page 12 for cohesion in writing).

_____

Lord Neptune, by Judith Nicholls

This poem comes from a collection of poems called *Dragonsfire* by Judith Nicholls. It is named after Neptune, who is the Roman god of the sea. The poem is about a father and his son at the seaside.

Build me a castle,
the young boy cried,
as he tapped his father's knee.
But make it tall
and make it wide,
with a king's throne just for me.

An echo drifted on the wind,
sang deep and wild and free:
Oh you can be king of the castle
but I am lord of the sea.

Give me your spade,
the father cried;
let's see what we can do!
We'll make it wide
so it holds the tide,
with a fine throne just for you.

He dug deep down
in the firm damp sand,
for the tide was falling fast.
The moat was deep,
the ramparts high,
and the turrets tall and vast.

Now I am king,
the young boy cried,
and this is my golden throne!
I rule the sands,
I rule the seas;
I'm lord of all lands, alone!

The sand-king ruled
from his golden court
and it seemed the wind had died;
but at dusk his throne
sank gently down
in Neptune's rolling tide.

And an echo rose upon the wind,
sang deep and wild and free:
Oh you may be king of the castle
but I am lord of the sea.

Lord Neptune, by Judith Nicholls

1. What does the boy want his father to do?
   _____

2. Whose voice can be heard on the wind?
   _____

3. List **four** things mentioned in the poem that might be found in a castle.

   a. _____

   b. _____

   c. _____

   d. _____

4. What happens to the boy's castle and when?
   _____
   _____

5. Look at the last two verses. What do you think this poem says about the power of nature?
   _____
   _____
   _____
   _____

Vocabulary in Action

Find and copy a line in the fifth verse that is an example of hyperbole (see page 40 for figurative language).

_____

Walk Two Moons, by Sharon Creech

This extract is from a novel by Sharon Creech, an award-winning author from the USA. In the story, Salamanca Hiddle is about to set off on an important road trip with her grandparents to find her missing mother.

My grandparents Hiddle are my father's parents, and they are full up to the tops of their heads with goodness and sweetness, and mixed in with all that goodness and sweetness is a large dash of peculiarity. This combination makes them interesting to know, but you can never predict what they will do or say.

Once it was settled that the three of us would go, the journey took on an alarming, expanding need to hurry that was like a walloping, great thundercloud assembling around me. During the week before we left, the sound of the wind was *hurry, hurry, hurry*, and at night even the silent darkness whispered *rush, rush, rush*. I did not think we would ever leave, and yet I did not want to leave. I did not really expect to survive the trip.

But I had decided to go and I would go, and I had to be there by my mother's birthday. This was extremely important. I believed that if there was any chance of bringing my mother back home it would happen on her birthday. If I had said this aloud to my father or to my grandparents, they would have said that I might as well try to catch a fish in the air, so I did not say it aloud. But I believed it. Sometimes I am as ornery and stubborn as an old donkey. My father says I lean on broken reeds and will get a face full of swamp mud one day.

When, at last, Gram and Gramps Hiddle and I set out that first day of the trip, I clutched seven good-luck charms and prayed for the first thirty minutes solid. I prayed that we would not be in an accident (I was terrified of cars and buses) and that we would get there by my mother's birthday – seven days away – and that we would bring her home. Over and over, I prayed the same thing. I prayed to trees. This was easier than praying directly to God. There was nearly always a tree nearby.

As we pulled onto the Ohio Turnpike, which is the flattest, straightest piece of road in God's whole creation, Gram interrupted my prayers. "Salamanca –"

I should explain right off that my real name is Salamanca Tree Hiddle. Salamanca, my parents thought, was the name of the Indian tribe to which my great-great grandmother belonged. My parents were mistaken. The name of the tribe was Seneca, but since my parents did not discover their error until after I was born and they were, by then, used to my name, it remained Salamanca.

My middle name, Tree, comes from your basic tree, a thing of such beauty to my mother that she made it part of my name. She wanted to be more specific and use Sugar Maple Tree, her very favourite because Sugar Maple is part of her own name, but Salamanca Sugar Maple Tree Hiddle sounded a bit much.

My mother used to call me Salamanca, but after she left, only my grandparents Hiddle called me Salamanca (when they were not calling me chickabiddy). To most other people, I was Sal, and to a few boys who thought they were especially amusing, I was Salamander.

In the car, as we started our long journey to Lewiston, Idaho, my grandmother Hiddle said, "Salamanca, why don't you entertain us?"

"What sort of thing do you have in mind?" I hoped they would not expect me to do something thumpingly embarrassing, like climb on top of the car and sing a little ditty. You can never tell with my grandparents.

But Gramps said, "How about a story? Spin us a yarn."

I certainly do know heaps of stories, but I learned most of them from Gramps. Gram suggested I tell one about my mother. That, I could not do. I had just reached the point where I could stop thinking about her every minute of every day. I wasn't ready – or at least I did not think I was ready – to talk about her.

Gramps said, "Well, then, what about your friends? You got any tales to tell about them?"

Instantly, Phoebe Winterbottom came to mind. There was certainly a hog's bellyful of things to tell about her. "I could tell you an extensively strange story," I warned.

"Oh, good!" Gram said. "Delicious!"

And that is how I happened to suspend my tree prayers and tell them about Phoebe Winterbottom, her disappearing mother, and the lunatic. It was also how I discovered that beneath Phoebe's story was another story.

Walk Two Moons, by Sharon Creech

1 Salamanca's grandparents have a combination of characteristics. Circle the **two** adjectives that Salamanca thinks this combination makes them.

peculiar   good   interesting   sweet   unpredictable

2 Look at the second paragraph. Find and copy **one** simile that describes how the upcoming journey feels to Salamanca.

_____

3 What does Salamanca want to do on her mother's birthday?

_____

4 Why doesn't Salamanca tell her father or grandparents what she believes about her mother's birthday? Tick **one**.

Because they have brought her a surprise gift. ☐

Because they think it is unlikely to happen. ☐

Because she does not trust her grandparents. ☐

Because she enjoys keeping secrets. ☐

5 *My father says I lean on broken reeds and will get a face full of swamp mud one day.* Using your own words, explain what Salamanca's father means.

_____

_____

6 *... the flattest, straightest piece of road in God's whole creation ...* What is this group of words an example of? Tick **one**.

personification ☐

alliteration ☐

simile ☐

hyperbole ☐

7 a. What mistake did Salamanca's parents make with her name?

_____

_____

b. Why did Salamanca's mother choose 'Tree' as her daughter's middle name?

_____

_____

8 Who is Salamanca's friend?

_____

9 How does Salamanca feel about her mother? Explain your answer using evidence from the text.

_____

_____

_____

_____

10 Do you think Salamanca will find her mother? Explain your answer using evidence from the text.

_____

_____

Grammar in Action

But I had decided to go and I would go, and I had to be there by my mother's birthday.

Circle the modal verb and underline the past perfect verb form in this sentence (see page 8 for modal verbs and page 14 for the perfect forms).

I Am Malala, by Malala Yousafzai with Patricia McCormick

This extract is from a book called 'I Am Malala', which tells the remarkable true story of a family uprooted by violence, the fight for girls' education and a young girl missing her old life in her homeland.

When I close my eyes, I can see my bedroom. The bed is unmade, my fluffy blanket in a heap, because I've rushed out for school, late for an exam. My school timetable is open on my desk to a page dated 9 October, 2012. And my school uniform – my white *shalwar* and blue *kamiz* – is on a peg on the wall, waiting for me.

I can hear the kids playing cricket in the alley behind our home. I can hear the hum of the bazaar not far away. And if I listen very closely I can hear Safina, my friend next door, tapping on the wall we share so she can tell me a secret.

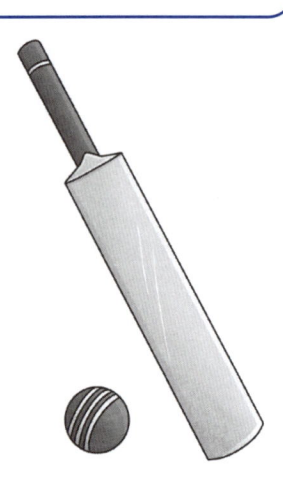

I smell rice cooking as my mother works in the kitchen. I hear my little brothers fighting over the remote – the TV switching between *WWE Smackdown* and cartoons. Soon, I'll hear my father's deep voice as he calls out my nickname. '*Jani*,' he'll say, which is Persian for 'dear one', 'how was the school running today?' He was asking how things were at the Khushal School for Girls, which he founded and I attended, but I always took the opportunity to answer the question literally.

'*Aha*,' I'd joke, 'the school is walking not running!' This was my way of telling him I thought things could be better.

I left that beloved home in Pakistan one morning – planning to dive back under the covers as soon as school was over – and ended up a world away.

Some people say it is too dangerous to go back there now. That I'll never be able to return. And so, from time to time, I go there in my mind.

But now another family lives in that home, another girl sleeps in that bedroom – while I am thousands of miles away. I don't care much about the other things in my room but I do worry about the school trophies on my bookcase. I even dream about them sometimes. There's a runner's-up award from the first speaking contest I ever entered. And more than forty-five golden cups and medals for being first in my class for exams, debates and competitions. To someone else, they might seem mere trinkets made of plastic. To someone else, they may simply look like prizes for good grades. But to me, they are reminders of the life I loved and the girl I was – before I left home that fateful day.

When I open my eyes, I am in my new bedroom. It is in a sturdy brick house in a damp and chilly place called Birmingham, England. Here there is water running from every tap, hot or cold as you like. No need to carry canisters of gas from the market to heat the water. Here there are large rooms with shiny wood floors, filled with large furniture and a large, large TV.

There is hardly a sound in this calm, leafy suburb. No children laughing and yelling. No women downstairs chopping vegetables and gossiping with my mother. No men smoking cigarettes and debating politics. Sometimes, though, even with these thick walls between us, I can hear someone in my family crying for home. But then my father will burst through the front door, his voice booming. '*Jani!*' he'll say. 'How was school today?'

Now there's no play on words. He's not asking about the school he runs and that I attend. But there's a note of worry in his voice, as if he fears I won't be there to reply. Because it was not so long ago that I was nearly killed – simply because I was speaking out about my right to go to school.

It was the most ordinary of days. I was fifteen, in Grade 9, and I'd stayed up far too late the night before studying for an exam.

I'd already heard the cock crow at dawn but had fallen back to sleep. I'd heard the morning call to prayer from the mosque nearby, but managed to hide under my quilt. And I'd pretended not to hear my father come to wake me.

Then my mother came and gently shook my shoulder.

"Wake up, *Pisho*," she said, calling me 'kitten' in Pashto, the language of the Pashtun people. "It's 7:30 a.m. and you're late for school!"

I had an exam on Pakistani studies. So I said a quick prayer to God. "If it is your will, may I please come first?" I whispered. "Oh, and thank you for all my success so far!"

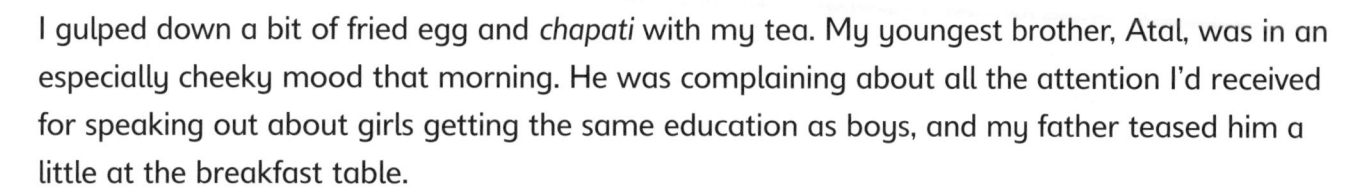

I gulped down a bit of fried egg and *chapati* with my tea. My youngest brother, Atal, was in an especially cheeky mood that morning. He was complaining about all the attention I'd received for speaking out about girls getting the same education as boys, and my father teased him a little at the breakfast table.

"When Malala is Prime Minister someday, you can be her secretary," he said.

Atal, the little clown in the family, pretended to be cross.

"No!" he cried. "She will be *my* secretary!"

All this banter nearly made me late and I raced out of the door, my half-eaten breakfast still on the table. I ran down the lane just in time to see the school bus crammed with other girls on their way to school. I jumped in that Tuesday morning and never looked back at my home.

I Am Malala, by Malala Yousafzai with Patricia McCormick

1 Name **two** things that Malala can remember hearing inside her old home when she closes her eyes.

a. _____

b. _____

2 *... He was asking how things were at the Khushal School for Girls, which he founded and I attended ...*

Circle the phrase closest in meaning to the phrase from the text.

a. he founded	he built	he started	he went to
b. I attended	I built	I started	I went to

3 In your own words, explain why Malala told her father that her school was 'walking not running'.

_____

_____

4 What did Malala win so many first prizes for?

_____

5 Why are her school trophies the only things Malala still worries about? Tick **one**.

They were prizes for good grades. ☐

They were lots of plastic cups and medals. ☐

They were achievements that she was proud of. ☐

6 a. In which city is Malala living in the present?

_____

b. In which country did Malala used to live?

_____

7 Malala describes several differences between her new and old homes. Find and copy some phrases into the blank boxes to show how different they are.

New home	Old home
water running from every tap, hot or cold as you like	
no children laughing or yelling	
	the hum of the bazaar not far away

8 **a.** On which date was Malala nearly killed?

_____

b. Why was she nearly killed?

_____

9 Malala describes how she 'left home that fateful day'.

Thinking about the whole extract, what does the word 'fateful' mean here? Circle **one**.

eventful   life-changing   terrible   important

10 Read from *I'd already heard the cock crow* ... to the end of the text. Tick the sentence that best summarises this part of the text.

Malala wakes up.   ☐

Malala eats breakfast.   ☐

Malala gets ready for school.   ☐

Malala is a secretary.   ☐

Punctuation in Action

Find and copy an example of parenthesis from the text, including the punctuation (see page 22 for parentheses) from the fifth paragraph.

_____

Jia-Wen's Grandad, by Matt Goodfellow

This poem comes from a modern collection of poems called *The Same Inside*. The poem describes a visit to a school by a pupil's grandad. It shows another pupil's reaction before, during and after the visit to show how their feelings about the visit change.

Jia-Wen's grandad came into school
to show our class his paintings.

Before he arrived, me and Barney
were moaning: "He can't even

speak English – what can we learn?"
He sat down, opened his satchel

and passed his pictures around.
Our fingers traced along strong

black horizons. Hands swept across
mountain peaks, through neat

little villages and over glittering oceans.
I stared into the eyes of a snarling dragon

surrounded by flames. Jia-Wen's grandad
never even spoke. Just packed up his pictures

gave Jia-Wen a kiss – and was gone.
That night, lying in bed, I heard

wind chimes in bamboo forests, watched
thin smoke-wisps melt into stars

and somewhere deep
in the distance of my dreams

I fire-danced with dragons.

Jia-Wen's Grandad, by Matt Goodfellow

1) Why does Jia-Wen's grandad visit the school?
   _____

2) Why are the poet and his friend Barney not looking forward to his visit?
   _____
   _____

3) Describe the paintings in your own words.
   _____
   _____

4) What does Jia-Wen's grandad **not** do at any point?
   _____

5) Do you think the poet enjoyed Jia-Wen's grandad's visit? Tick **one**.

   Yes ☐   No ☐

   Explain why.
   _____
   _____
   _____

Vocabulary in Action

Find and copy some examples of imagery that use the following senses (see page 40 for figurative language).

a. sight _____

b. sound _____

c. touch _____

The House with Chicken Legs, by Sophie Anderson

> This story is inspired by Slavic folklore about Baba Yaga: a supernatural woman who lives in the forest. At the beginning of the book, we meet Marinka, who lives with her grandmother in a rather unusual house.

My house has chicken legs. Two or three times a year, without warning, it stands up in the middle of the night and walks away from where we've been living. It might walk a hundred miles or it might walk a thousand, but where it lands is always the same. A lonely, bleak place at the edge of civilisation.

It nestles in dark forbidden woods, rattles on windswept icy tundra, and hides in crumbling ruins at the far edge of cities. At this moment it's perched on a rocky ledge high in some barren mountains. We've been here two weeks and I still haven't seen anyone living. Dead people, I've seen plenty of those of course. They come to visit Baba and she guides them through The Gate. But the real, live, living people, they all stay in the town and villages far below us.

Maybe if it was summer a few of them would wander up here, to picnic and look at the view. They might smile and say hello. Someone my own age might visit – maybe a whole group of children. They might stop near the stream and splash in the water to cool off. Perhaps they would invite me to join them.

"How's the fence coming?" Baba calls through the open window, pulling me from my daydream.

"Nearly done." I wedge another thigh bone into the low stone wall. Usually I sink the bones straight into the earth, but up here the ground is too rocky, so I built a knee-high stone wall all the way around the house, pushed the bones into it and balanced the skulls on top. But it keeps collapsing in the night. I don't know if it's the wind, or wild animals, or clumsy dead people, but every day we've been here I've had to rebuild a part of the fence.

Baba says the fence is important to keep out the living and guide in the dead, but that's not why I fix it. I like to work with the bones because my parents would have touched them once, long ago, when they built fences and guided the dead. Sometimes I think I feel the warmth of their hands lingering on the cold bones, and I imagine what it might have been like to hold my parents for real. This makes my heart lift and ache all at the same time.

The house creaks loudly and leans over until the front window is right above me. Baba pokes her head out and smiles. "Lunch is ready. I've made a feast of *shchi* and black bagels. Enough for Jack too."

My stomach rumbles as the smell of cabbage soup and freshly baked bread hits my nose. "Just the gate hinge, then I'm done." I lift up a foot bone, wire it back into place, and look around for Jack.

He's picking at a weathered piece of rock underneath a dried-up heather bush, probably hoping to find a woodlouse or a beetle. "Jack!" I call and he tilts his head up. One of his silver eyes flashes as it catches the light. He bounds towards me in an ungainly cross between flying and jumping, lands on my shoulder, and tries to push something into my ear.

"Get off!" My hand darts up to cover my ear. Jack's always stashing food to save for later. I don't know why he thinks my ears are a good hiding place. He forces the thing into my fingers instead; something small, dry and crispy. I pull my hand down to look. It's a crumpled, broken spider.

"Thanks, Jack." I drop the carcass into my pocket. I know he means well, sharing his food, but I've had enough of dead things. "Come on." I shake my head and sigh. "Baba's made a feast. For two people and a jackdaw."

I turn and look at the town far below us. All those houses, snuggled close together, keeping each other company in this cold and lonely place. I wish my house was a normal house, down there, with the living. I wish my family was a normal family, too. But my house has chicken legs, and my grandmother is a Yaga and a Guardian of The Gate between this world and the next. So my wishes are as hollow as the skulls of the fence.

The House with Chicken Legs, by Sophie Anderson

1. Look at the first paragraph. What is unusual about the house? Give **two** examples.

   a. _____

   b. _____

2. Why does Marinka see plenty of dead people? Explain your answer in detail using evidence from the text.

   _____

   _____

   _____

3. What **three** things does Marinka use to build the fence around the house?

   _____

4. Why does Marinka rebuild the fence every day? Give **two** reasons and explain your answers using evidence from the text.

   _____

   _____

   _____

5. What is *shchi*?

   _____

6. What kind of an animal is Jack? Tick **one**.

   a woodlouse ☐

   a bird ☐

   a spider ☐

   a beetle ☐

7 *... my wishes are as hollow as the skulls of the fence ...*

    a. What type of figurative language is this? Tick **one**.

    metaphor ☐   alliteration ☐   simile ☐   personification ☐

    b. Explain in your own words what the figurative language means.

    _____

8 How do you know that Marinka and Jack are friends?

_____

9 Draw lines to match each word to its word class and its meaning.

bleak	verb	unwelcoming
ungainly	noun	to be slow to disappear
lingering	adjective	the dead body of an animal
carcass	adjective	awkward

10 Thinking about the whole extract, how does Marinka feel about her life? Give **two** feelings and use evidence from the text to explain your answer.

_____

_____

_____

_____

Spelling in Action

Underline the base word in each of these words (see page 30 for base words).

civilisation   rebuild   normal   warning   forbidden

Magic of Jinn, by Stephen Krensky and Giles Clare

This non-fiction text is about supernatural beings called genies or 'jinn'. It describes different types of genies from folklore and explains that genies are still popular characters in modern culture.

Genies in folklore

Jinn, also called genies, are supernatural beings with great magical powers, who might be good or evil. 'Jinn' is an Arabic word, and male and female jinn have appeared for thousands of years in Arabian cultures ranging from northern Africa across to Persia in western Asia. Wherever they live, jinn are hard to pin down because they can take so many forms.

Jann

An early form of jinn, these shapeshifters fit in well with their desert surroundings by taking the form of either a whirlwind or a white camel. Jann also have the power to replenish oases that have dried up, and so it makes sense for thirsty desert travellers to stay on their good side.

Marid

The most powerful of all jinn, Marids can grant wishes to people, but won't do so without a good reason. (Being imprisoned within a lamp, for example, is considered a good reason.) While most Marids look quite human, the Bahamut, a Marid mentioned in the Islamic religious book the Quaran, is a giant fish.

Hinn

The Hinn are closely related to jinn in Arabic folklore. They like to take the shape of dogs, though sometimes they choose other animals to imitate. This ability to transform allows them to wander freely among towns and villages without being noticed.

Nasnas

This jinn from Arabic folklore is hard to miss. The Nasnas looks like a human being cut in half from top to bottom, with one arm, one leg, half a head, and half a body. Not surprisingly, it gets around by hopping on its one foot.

Genies in modern popular culture

Despite their roots in folklore, genies still frequently appear as characters in modern popular culture from books to TV and films, to video games and songs. There is a huge, all-powerful genie called Asif in the children's novel, *Dragon Rider*, by Cornelia Funke; the Pokémon Hoopa is a djinn Pokémon, who can grant wishes with its rings; there are two genies in the video game, *Sonic and the Secret Rings*, one good, one bad; and *Genie in a Bottle* was the name of a hit song from Christina Aguilera's first pop album.

Perhaps the most famous genie in modern popular culture is the 'Genie of the Lamp', who appears in the Disney animation of *Aladdin* (1992) and the live-action remake (2019). The former featured the voice of Robin Williams and the latter starred Will Smith as the genie. In both cases, the character of the genie is certainly a lot friendlier and more humorous than the genies of folklore. In fact, genies nowadays are often portrayed as powerful but benevolent, aiding the hero on their quest. These modern portrayals also tend to focus on the central idea of the genie's ability to grant three wishes.

The films of Aladdin are based on a story called *Aladdin and his Wonderful Lamp*, which appears in a collection of folk tales from the Middle East called *One Thousand and One Nights*. The story and the films are similar but do have some differences. Firstly, in the folk tale, Aladdin is from China and he lives with both his parents. Secondly, there is no Abu the monkey in the folk tale and no magic carpet. Thirdly, there is an evil sorcerer in both the films and story, but Jafar only appears in the films. In the story, the evil sorcerer is from Africa and doesn't have a name. In the film, Aladdin tricks Jafar and traps him in the magic lamp, whereas in the story, he tricks him into drinking a poison that kills him instantly. There are not one but two genies in the original story. The genie of the lamp has little personality and only really appears to grant wishes, but a second, less powerful genie lives in Aladdin's magic ring and is his companion.

Magic of Jinn, by Stephen Krensky and Giles Clare

1 Which language does the word 'jinn' come from?

_____

2 The statements in this table are about the characteristics of jinn. Tick to show whether each one is true or false.

Statement	True	False
Jinn can be male or female.		
Some jinn can change form to fit in with their surroundings.		
Jinn are always evil.		
All jinn are from North Africa.		

3 In your own words, explain why desert travellers might want to stay on the Jann's 'good side'.

_____

_____

_____

_____

4 According to mythology, what do Hinn take the shape of?

_____

5 Why does a Nasnas hop around?

_____

6 Which type of jinn is the most powerful? Circle **one**.

Jann   Hinn   Nasnas   Marid

7 Look at the paragraph beginning *Perhaps the most famous* …. Which word is closest in meaning to 'benevolent'? Tick **one**.

- merciful ☐
- kind ☐
- smart ☐
- mean ☐

8 Where does the story of Aladdin come from originally?

_____

9 Complete this table to show the differences between the original and the modern versions of *Aladdin*. Parts of two have been done for you.

	Original story	Modern film versions
Jinn		There is one genie of the lamp.
The fate of the enemy		Aladdin traps Jafar in the lamp.
Other characters		

10 Give **one** difference between the jinn of folklore and genies in modern popular culture. Explain your answer using evidence from the text.

_____

_____

Spelling in Action

Underline the homophone or near homophone that is used incorrectly (see page 28 for homophones and near homophones), then write the correct spelling.

… these shapeshifters fit in well with their dessert surroundings by taking the form of either a whirlwind or a white camel.

_____

Medusa and Minotaur Take Tea, by Rachel Piercey

This poem comes from a modern collection of poems called *Falling Out of the Sky*. It is about two terrifying monsters from Greek mythology. Medusa is famous because people turned to stone if they looked straight at her. The Minotaur ate people sent into the maze it lived in. In this poem, they are having tea together.

The china is in smithereens
before our tea has even brewed
but it hardly matters.
Minotaur is half bull
and a little clumsy
but bigger things have been shattered,
like our reputations,
and we are here with pen and paper
to set the record straight.

We blame the poets
and the storytellers
and the kings playing at war
who wanted this head and that head,
this pesky soldier
and that far-off monster dead.
Often they didn't even leave their thrones.

'I didn't even like the taste
of human flesh, but it was all they sent
into the Labyrinth,' lows Minotaur.
I write this down,
and also that I didn't choose
to have a head of thrashing snakes,
to turn everyone who looks at me to stone.

The poets didn't care to judge
the malice heaped on us
by petty gods,
just how we ended up
and our ability to finish off
their 'heroes' Perseus and Theseus,
men we'd never heard of,
coming with swords and shields to kill us.

Wouldn't *you* put up a fight?
But of course it was useless.
In stories, monsters always die.

I get some sturdier mugs and pour the tea.
My hair hisses and seethes.
Minotaur asks me to write down
that we were lonely.

Medusa and Minotaur Take Tea, by Rachel Piercey

1 *The china is in smithereens*

What has happened to the china?

_____

2 Medusa and Minotaur want to 'set the record straight'. What does this mean?

_____

_____

3 Name the **three** types of people Medusa and Minotaur blame for their reputations.

_____

4 *Often they didn't even leave their thrones.*

What impression do you get of the kings from this line?

_____

_____

5 Look at the first three verses of the poem. What is unusual about how Medusa and Minotaur look? Find and copy groups of words from the poem as evidence.

Medusa: _____

Minotaur: _____

6 How do Medusa and Minotaur justify their actions? Explain your answer using evidence from the text.

_____

_____

_____

7 Look at the fourth verse. Find a word that has:

   a. the same meaning as 'hatred'. _____

   b. the opposite meaning to 'important'. _____

8 Why does the poet put inverted commas around the word 'heroes'?

_____

_____

9 Look at the whole poem. How do you think Medusa and Minotaur are feeling? Explain your answer using evidence from the text.

_____

_____

_____

_____

10 Which of these statements best describes the effect of this poem? Tick **two**.

It makes you feel proud of people who try to get rid of bad things in the world. ☐

It makes you feel angry that some people ruin other people's lives. ☐

It makes you feel sorry for people who are unfairly attacked. ☐

It makes you feel it is important to listen to different points of view. ☐

Spelling in Action

I get some sturdier mugs and pour the tea.

Here are some homophones of the word 'pour' (see page 28 for homophones and near homophones). What do they mean? Use a dictionary to help.

   a. poor (adjective) _____

   b. pore (noun) _____

Primary Practice **English Year 5**

Writing skills: My Mythical Relative

The Writing skills task is inspired by the themes in the reading comprehension texts. It provides an opportunity to apply the skills practised in this book. Answer guidance can be downloaded from the **Schofield & Sims** website.

Amazingly, one of your relatives is one of the mythical creatures from this book! Use your imagination to write a biography of this mythical family member. You might choose Baba Yaga, one of the jinn, Medusa or the Minotaur. Write about their early life and school, their job, their favourite memories and their personality. Alternatively, you could write about one of your real relatives. Use the prompt below to begin your biography if you wish to.

You could use some of the following in your biography:
- relative clauses (page 6)
- cohesion in writing (page 12)
- the perfect forms (page 14)
- parentheses (page 22)
- suffixes (pages 36 and 38).

Re-read 'The House with Chicken Legs' (page 68), 'Magic of Jinn' (page 72) and 'Medusa and Minotaur Take Tea' (page 76) for some ideas.

My grandmother Medusa was born thousands of years ago in Greece.

_____

_____

_____

_____

_____

_____

_____

_____

Tip When you have finished writing, remember to proofread your story and correct any missing punctuation and spelling mistakes.

Final practice

The Final practice includes grammar, punctuation, spelling, vocabulary and reading comprehension questions. Work through the questions carefully and try to answer each one. The target time for completing these questions is 45 minutes. The answers can be downloaded from the **Schofield & Sims** website.

1) Circle the present perfect or past perfect verb forms in each sentence.

  a. Georgie has gone to stay at her stepfather's house.

  b. The pirate ship had sunk with all its treasure on board.

  c. Haven't we seen this film before?

  d. Marlon had never flown in an aeroplane before.

1 mark

2) Underline the **two** adverbials in this sentence.

After school, Samir and I decided that it would be funny to hide behind a tree.

1 mark

3) Tick to show whether the underlined words are a main clause or a relative clause.

Sentence	Main clause	Relative clause
a. My grandmother, <u>whose family came from South America</u>, enjoys playing the guitar on her patio.		
b. <u>This old book,</u> which I found in the attic, <u>is full of adventure stories from around the world.</u>		
c. Whenever our teacher is pleased, <u>he dances around the classroom and sings.</u>		
d. I was excited about going to the theme park that <u>had just opened near our house.</u>		

1 mark

4) Insert **two** brackets in the correct places in this sentence.

Our netball team won by a single goal today it was twelve-all until the very last minute.

1 mark

Final practice

5 Rewrite this sentence using the correct spellings of the adjectives.

The ambicious explorer searched for spetial treasures while fighting ferotious enemies.

_____

_____

1 mark

6 Draw lines to match each prefix to the correct word.

dis		lead
de		rail
mis		courage

1 mark

7 Tick to show where the commas should go in this sentence. Tick **three**.

Late last night my sister who is scared of the dark thought she saw a ghost.

☐ ☐ ☐ ☐ ☐

1 mark

8 Write the correct relative pronoun to complete each sentence.

a. My skateboard, _____ is red and white, snapped in half last week.

b. Those clothes _____ are too small for you are going to the charity shop.

c. Jack's cousin, _____ is scared of thunder, never goes out in a storm.

1 mark

9 Circle the subject and underline the object in this sentence.

A lot of children play sport at after-school clubs.

1 mark

Final practice

10 Tick to show which sentence uses dashes correctly. Tick **one**.

He turned up – late in his old suit of course and – spilt soup on the king. ☐

He turned up late – in his old suit of course – and spilt soup on the king. ☐

He turned up late in his old suit – of course and spilt soup on the king. ☐

He turned up late in his old suit – of course and spilt soup – on the king. ☐

1 mark

11 Underline the correct spellings of the **two** homophones in this sentence.

When his mobile phone went off, Will had to **desert / dessert** his friend Simon before he had finished his **desert / dessert**.

1 mark

12 Underline the **two** modal verbs in this sentence.

If you have a headache, you ought to rest and you should feel better.

1 mark

13 Tick to show which sentence is written in the present perfect tense. Tick **one**.

Due to the storm, the ferry is delayed by two hours. ☐

Due to the storm, the ferry will be delayed by two hours. ☐

Due to the storm, the ferry has been delayed by two hours. ☐

Due to the storm, the ferry had been delayed by two hours. ☐

1 mark

14 Rewrite this sentence using **three** commas in the correct places.

Although it was a cold frosty morning Sarah decided to go for a long brisk walk around the park.

_____

_____

1 mark

15 Circle the **two** adverbs of possibility in this sentence.

He was certainly going too fast, which perhaps caused him to fall off his bike.

1 mark

Final practice

The Depths of the World, by Michael Johnstone

> On 23rd January 1960, Jacques Piccard and Don Walsh set out to explore part of the Earth that had never been visited by humans before. They were going to use a vehicle called a bathyscaphe to dive to the deepest place in the world – the bottom of the Marianas Trench in the Pacific Ocean.

The lowest point in the world – 11 kilometres below the ocean's surface – that was the goal of Swiss scientist Jacques Piccard. An experienced diver, Piccard had made many trips in his special underwater craft, called the *Trieste*, but never before had he attempted to venture so deep.

Piccard had worked for years to help his father, Auguste Piccard, to develop and perfect the *Trieste*. This was to be its toughest test – the craft would be underwater for more than nine hours.

The weather was rough and stormy on the day of the descent. It had already taken four days for a United States Navy tugboat to tow the *Trieste* to a point above the *Marianas Trench*, and the *Trieste* had been damaged along the way.

But Piccard and his fellow crewman, a US Naval Officer called Don Walsh, decided to go ahead with the attempt, rather than face months of delay waiting for another opportunity.

Most of the *Trieste* consisted of a huge metal hull, called the float, which was partly filled with iron pellets that helped it to sink.

Hanging beneath the float was a small round cabin, just large enough to hold two people and the craft's controls, with large viewing windows.

At 8:23 a.m., the two men climbed into the tiny cabin and Piccard opened the hatches to allow water to flow into the float. The *Trieste* slipped quickly underneath the waves. Very carefully Piccard adjusted the flow of water into the hull, until the machine was descending at just less than a metre a second.

By 800 metres down, the water around the *Trieste* was chilly and completely dark. There was no sign of life.

At a depth of 10 kilometres, the silence was suddenly shattered by a loud splintering. The *Trieste* began to tremble. As Piccard reported later, he did not know what to do. Everything on board seemed normal. "Let us go on," he finally said.

At 12:56 p.m., Piccard and Walsh saw the ocean floor appear on their depth finder, which showed how far they were from the bottom.

Final practice

It took them 10 long minutes to travel that short distance. Then, at last, as Piccard stated, "At 13:06 hours the *Trieste* made a perfect landing. In the name of science and humanity, we took possession of the abyss, the last extreme on our Earth that remained to be conquered."

The two men gazed in wonder at the still world outside. The floor of the ocean was made of ivory-coloured dust, like talcum powder.

They watched as a large flat fish slowly swam away into the dark. For many years scientists had wanted to find out if fish could exist deep in the ocean. Now, in one glance, the debate was settled.

Walsh telephoned the surface to confirm their depth and then discovered what had caused the bang. One of the large viewing windows had cracked, but was withstanding the water pressure.

After 20 minutes Piccard let loose a shower of iron pellets and the *Trieste* began to float upwards. Gradually their speed increased.

At 600 metres below the surface, light began to filter through the waves. And at 4:56 p.m. the *Trieste* burst safely back into the open air, exactly on schedule.

Piccard's descent to the depths had lasted just a few hours, yet in that short time he had conquered the world's last frontier – the very bottom of the sea.

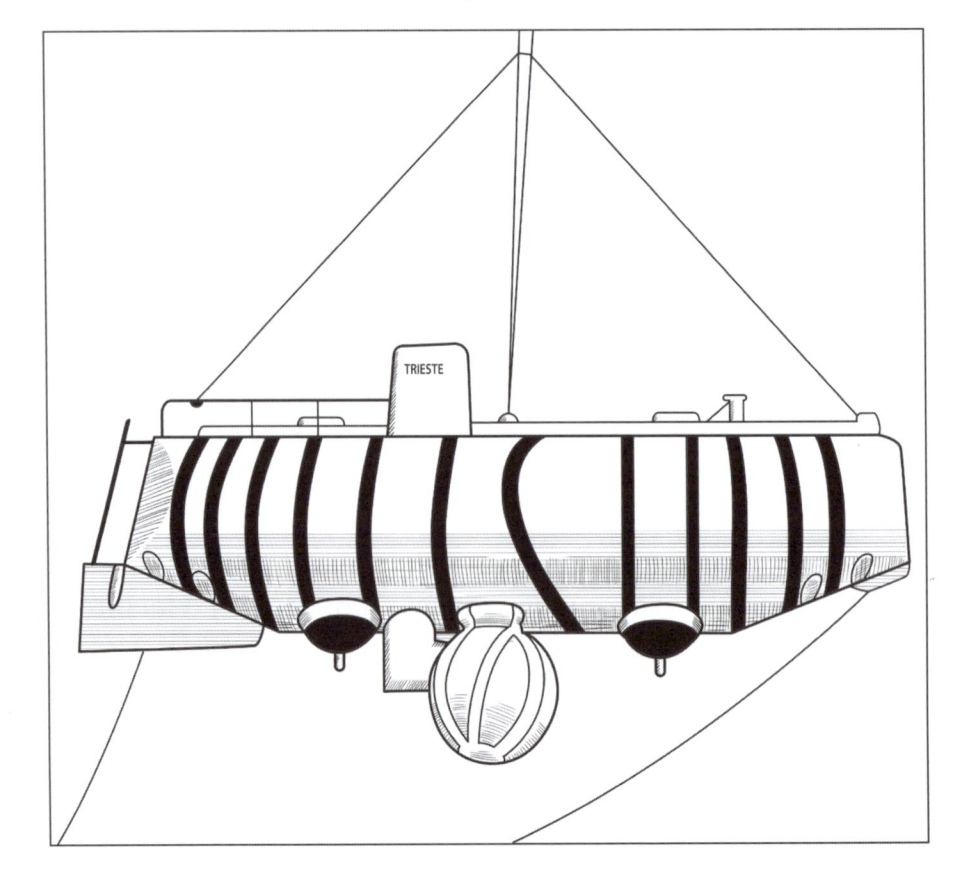

Final practice

16 What and where is the deepest place on Earth?

_____

1 mark

17 The *Trieste* consisted of two parts. What were they called?

_____ and _____

1 mark

18 Name **two** things that helped the *Trieste* to sink.

a. _____

b. _____

1 mark

19 Look at the paragraph beginning *At 8:23 a.m., ...* . Find and copy **one** word that means 'going down'.

_____

1 mark

20 Approximately how long did the journey to the bottom of the trench take? Tick **one**.

9 hours ☐

5 hours ☐

2 hours ☐

10 hours ☐

1 mark

21 Why might Piccard and Walsh have abandoned their attempt before or during the journey down? Give **two** reasons and explain your answer using evidence from the text.

_____

_____

_____

2 marks

Primary Practice **English Year 5**

Final practice

22 How did Piccard and Walsh know they were near the bottom?

_____

1 mark

23 Draw lines to match the words from the text to their meanings.

abyss		resisting successfully
frontier		pass through
withstanding		the furthest place to have been discovered
filter		an extremely deep hole

2 marks

24 What 'debate was settled' on the ocean floor?

_____

1 mark

25 Explain how the *Trieste* got back up to the surface.

_____

_____

2 marks

26 How do you think Piccard's feelings changed during their journey? Give **one** change and explain your answer using evidence from the text.

_____

_____

_____

_____

2 marks

Total:

30 marks